£18·95

THE PRICE OF CHARITY

By the same author

Scarlet Pimpernel of the Vatican
Fred Karno – Master of Mirth and Tears

The Price of Charity

J.P. GALLAGHER

LONDON · ROBERT HALE

First published in Great Britain 1975

ISBN 0 7091 4735 X

Robert Hale & Company
Clerkenwell House
Clerkenwell Green
London EC1R OHT

Composed by Specialised Offset Services Ltd, Liverpool
and printed and bound in Great Britain by
Redwood Burn Limited
Trowbridge and Esher

CONTENTS

AUTHOR'S PREFACE

This book, imperfect in some respects as it may be, has taken nearly four years to assemble. During that time the number of registered charities in England and Wales alone rose from around 76,000 to more than 100,000, a fact which poses the problem of where to limit this analysis of where the money comes from, where it goes, and how well or otherwise it is administered.

It is a constantly changing picture, like a kaleidoscope held in a trembling hand. Anyone undertaking research into this vast subject finds it is not made easier by the odd mixture of pride, bias and reticence that distinguishes many charity officials and workers. Then there is the sheer complexity – sometimes deliberate – of some accounting procedures. Not deliberate in the same sense but equally baffling when it comes to drawing comparisons is the fact that the financial years of the different organizations vary widely: some run from January to December, others end in March each year, others in June, some in September, and so on.

Above all, when one discovers the enormousness of the scene, there is the question: where does one stop?

After realizing that as soon as I had produced a broad picture of the finances of British charity in a given year, the whole story changed to an extent within months and that any attempt to bring out, in 1974 say, a book that was accurate to the end of 1973 would be utterly impossible, I decided to confine almost all financial reporting to the years 1971 and 1972, for which there are now at least established and comparable figures. I suppose one might suggest that to bring things right up to date, the reader could add ten per cent to revenues and costs quoted for each year to today. That is a pretty constant pattern for the majority of important voluntary organizations.

Then there was the problem of which organizations should be dealt with in any detail. The final selection here forms a purely arbitrary personal choice of charities covering differing fields, since one could go on for ever. I have to apologize to the many deserving organizations that are not mentioned here – charities like the Spastics Society, Action for the Crippled Child, and the Samaritans, to name only three. There was a particular reason, however, for leaving out some of the largest charities. The book is intended to be limited so far as possible to organizations operating predominantly in the United Kingdom and in certain cases in Eire. That ruled out Oxfam and Christian Aid for example, charities which work mainly overseas.

It is of course customary in prefaces to acknowledge sources and the assistance received. Many sources are quoted in the book but so many people said that they could be more helpful and talk more freely if they were not identified that I decided to mention as few names as possible. I do have to thank scores of charity officials who granted sometimes lengthy interviews and most especially the Charity Commissioners and the Wells Organization for an immense amount of detailed information.

When friends and acquaintances first heard that I was 'writing a book on charity', the response was immediate, emotive, and sometimes funny. I was bombarded with anecdotes of 'rackets', accusations of waste and overlapping, of officials wallowing in luxury – all the prejudices that are discussed in their place in this book. I cannot remember anyone offering any praise to anyone or anything! Whether people 'love' the objects of charity or not, they certainly are vocal about money. But, working steadily through the list of complaints that I eventually made, I truly found very little that would stand up. The public is – as I was told at the beginning by impartial people such as Civil Servants involved in this area – thoroughly ignorant about charity work. Incidentally, those same Civil Servants and others were prepared to bet that a book on charity of the type I had outlined to them would never be finished!

I have tried to keep my personal conclusions to the minimum, preferring rather to provide facts on which readers may form their own judgements.

December 1974 *J.P. Gallagher*
Bickley, Kent

1

DEFINITELY CHRISTIAN?

Nobody can be certain exactly how much money goes today to charity in the United Kingdom, but it is *probable* that during 1973 something like £300 million went in donations, legacies and grants to more than 180,000 charities and churches and to research organizations and non-profit making associations of many, many kinds. In addition, Government grants to non-profit making and research organizations were likely to have been at least £500 million.

That total of £800 million devoted in one way or another to 'good works' in their broadest sense does not include the large but completely unguessable amount raised by the thousands of informal projects that go on all the time, such as pub and club collections and draws, coffee mornings, whist drives and similar events held for strictly local objectives and never reflected in official statistics of any kind.

Recorded assets of only 100 of the big fund-raising charities at the beginning of 1972 were £200,994,000 and the assets of only 50 of the major trusts or foundations were £712,717,000. On 1 January 1973, the Official Custodian for Charities held no less than £162,848,825 in sterling securities on behalf of various charities, mostly smaller concerns than the leading hundred.

Apart from the officially listed charities – and anything from one to two thousand are registered each year in England and Wales alone – there is an unknown number of organizations that have never bothered to enroll and there is an equally uncounted number of charity trading companies, some distinctly dubious. Charity is indeed Big Business.

It is as well to begin the story of charity in the United Kingdom with a definition, and we are in trouble from the start! The word charity comes from the Latin *caritat* (affection) and *carus* (dear, precious, high-priced). English dictionaries give as their prime definition 'Christian love' and it is true that charity is equatable with love and that in some modern Bible translations the word is replaced by 'love', as in St Paul's epistle: "Though I speak with the tongues of men and of angels and have not love. . . ." But it is to be noted that such dictionaries blithely ignore the Jews, Buddhists, Confucians, Islam – all the other world religions, not to mention agnosticism and atheism, most followers of which may be presumed to have as much love for mankind as many self-styled Christians, possibly more. Certainly, as we shall see later, the amount given by Britain's Jews in any one year to charitable causes in Israel equalled the combined revenue of the three largest United Kingdom charities.

The *Oxford English Dictionary* lists first 'Christian love, especially of our fellow men' and then goes on to such definitions as 'natural affection', 'benevolence to the poor', 'christianness', and eventually reaches 'almsgiving, acts of charity done to the poor; bequest, foundation, institute etc. for the benefit of others, especially the poor or helpless'. The *Encyclopaedia Britannica* defines charity as 'one of the oldest of Christian virtues, together with faith and hope', though it does refer the reader to 'Philanthropy', where he can find, at last, references to good works which include those practised by other religions and creeds. There is also the comment that such statements as 'I'm not longing for charity' emphasize the condescension with which charity is often shown!

The Jewish definition of charity is *tsedakah*, meaning 'righteousness', the Chinese 'compassionate good works', and the Japanese 'benevolent love'.

Of course charity is as old as history itself, stemming from the obligation to look after one's family and extend hospitality to strangers. Pharaoh sheltered the poor and distributed bread and clothing, Greek and Roman vagrants and beggars were under the protection of the gods, Xenophon endowed a foundation to provide food for all on festival days and surplus food from feasts was given to beggars. Roman beggars took their food directly from their patrons' dinner tables while Greek temples maintained inns for strangers and set up the original medical centres. A Roman citizen had the *right* to poor relief and the first recorded charitable foundation linked with the Roman poor was founded, possibly by Trajan, around the first century A.D. Buddhist monks have always tended the sick and in ancient China there were houses of refuge of various kinds and sick-visiting systems. One of the five obligatory duties in the Islamic world is to pay a tax from which money is distributed to the needy. Great hospitals were opened in places like Damascus (707 A.D.), Baghdad and Cairo.

In Britain also, care of the sick and poor was undertaken

by the nobles and, especially, by the monasteries. In 1540 about 750 hospitals were being run by monks in England. As far back as 1084 Lanfranc established two almshouses in Canterbury, while early hospitals such as St Bartholomew's (1123) and St Thomas's (1200) were combined almshouses, shelters for the sick and orphanages. By the Middle Ages merchants and craft guilds began to take over something of the role of the monasteries. The Reformation completely finished off the monasteries however, immediately throwing up a great increase in poverty and distress. King Henry VIII did not care about the effects on the poor but Queen Elizabeth I did and it was she who initiated systems of public relief, in her typical fashion.

She had no intention whatsoever of spending her own money, but told Dudley, Earl of Leicester that *he* was to found an almshouse. Dudley also saved his own money, for he went to Warwick and induced the townspeople to give him their guild-hall for the purpose. From then on the establishment of almshouses became fashionable with the nobles and rich merchants. People who escaped the plague set up pest-houses and orphanages out of gratitude. Over the centuries many followed their example, with almost as many different reasons – the tugs of conscience, the desire for immortality in stone, spiting relations by cutting them out of wills, tax avoidance, death duty reduction, and so on.

By the beginning of the seventeenth century there was such a great increase in vagrancy and destitution that the State had to step in and the Poor Law Act of 1601 laid upon local authorities the duty of providing from the rates for the sick, needy and homeless, establishing the principle that the care of such people was part of the social structure of the State. However, for the next 200 years or so the greatest help still came from private sources, and in 30 years of the eighteenth century nearly 60 voluntary hospitals were founded. The Industrial Revolution forced the State to take even more responsibility and embark on the long trail to the National Health Service Act of 1946.

The nineteenth century saw the beginning and tremendously swift development of voluntary organizations dedicated to scientific, cultural, medical, charitable and other causes. The Young Men's Christian Association was established in 1844, the Young Women's version in 1855, the Children's Aid Society in 1856, Howard League for Penal Reform in 1866, National Institute for the Blind in 1868, Mothers Union in 1876, Salvation Army in 1878. There followed associations like the Boys Brigade, Society for the Prevention of Cruelty to Children, the Soldiers and Sailors Families Association, and the National Trust. In the early twentieth century came the Scouts and Guides, Rotary, the National Federation of Women's Institutes, the British Legion, and, in 1930, Youth Hostels. Since World War II there has been a particular expansion of societies concerned with the welfare of both the young and the aged and with work for the physically handicapped in many areas.

'Charity' is an extremely emotive word and can prompt heated arguments, even among mild and benevolent old ladies, with people airing passionate preferences, vitriolic dislikes, anxieties and sometimes dark suspicions. There has grown up in Britain over recent years an extraordinary degree of reserve – to use the very weakest expression – towards charity. With a substantial proportion of the public there is positive hostility to the very idea. With some even the word 'charity' has become dirtied, associated with 'hippies', 'squatters', 'reds', uncomfortable propaganda and repugnant advertising. Nonetheless the money rolls in.

Some of the aspects of charity work most criticized, validly or otherwise, by the public and examined in this book are the proportion of money going to actual charitable work, professional fund-raisers, the cost of appeals and administration, charity trading, payment of commission to collectors, even payment of salaries at all to charity officials! There is a belief that quite a number of charities exist only for the welfare of their trustees, or someone like that, and widespread criticism of what are believed to be overlapping appeals and the proliferation of charities covering the same field, especially cancer.

A frequently voiced complaint is directed against charities operating from glamorous and apparently expensive London headquarters but in reality the facts are very different from what they seem. For example, it is true that the Spastics Society works from beautiful Park Crescent in London but its long lease from the Crown restricts the use of the offices to non-profit making bodies and the rent works out at less than £1 per square foot. The British Red Cross in Grosvenor Crescent has a similar Crown lease. Shelter calculates that its Strand offices, at about £2.50 a square foot are more than value for money because the centralized location means that they get the services of voluntary workers worth up to perhaps £20,000 a year. Several other charities which had central London headquarters have sold them, at substantial profits, and moved further out.

Above all there is questioning whether, with great changes in social conditions and the development of the Welfare State, there should be any need for private fund-giving to any person or organization. "Why should we do what the Government should be doing?" is the cry from many dwellers in the Paternal Society. This attitude also finds a reflection in some reactions to strikes and consequent forced wage rises in the public service sector – Christmas boxes dropped off catastrophically for refuse collectors and postmen after strife-torn 1970.

There are a number of reasons for taking a hard and as objective as possible look at charity but it should be said from the start that, by and large, the still prevalent image of most charities as 'Victorian', woolly and inefficient is becoming less and less true. Under economic and social pressures charity is doing a lot of spring-cleaning . . . and not before time. The *integrity* of genuine, registered charities is undoubted but the public is astonishingly uninformed – and therefore suspicious and cynical – and very often does not know what is a legitimate charity and what is not. Perfectly justified public criticism of the phonies and fringe operators rubs off most unfairly on *all* charity work. As for fund-raising costs and methods, the National Council of Social Service, which co-ordinates the work of some 130 charities and represents them at Government level, has said that there is an 'almost total lack' of public knowledge of the subject.

It is far from generally realized that there are huge gaps in the Welfare State which only charity can even attempt to fill. These gaps are widening, not shrinking. For there is the paradox that improvements in social conditions create a greater not lesser need for charity money and workers. Put simply, people today expect more for free . . . or for love! Higher standards of living mean that the 'standard of poverty' has changed also. Once soup kitchens were considered sufficient for the needy; today much, much more is demanded.

Supervising charity accounts in England and Wales are the Charity Commissioners, of whom much will be heard in this book. Their report for the year 1972 showed that there were then 80,834 charities on their register, plus a further 22,000 – most recreational – which had previously been under the control of the Department of Education and Science. In the year the Commissioners received 2,472 applications for registration, of which 1,006 were charities founded in 1972. The Commissioners accepted 2,219. A registered charity gets a 50 per cent rates rebate and may, at the discretion of the rating authority, get up to 100 per cent. Up to £50,000 donated to it is free of estate duty. It pays no taxes on its charitable income or assets.

Referring to the newly formed organizations registered during the year, the Commissioners compared the face of charity in Britain in 1876 with the 1970s. In 1876 the *total* income of endowed charities came to just over £2 million a year. Rather more than half that income went to the relief of poverty and sickness, about one-third went to education, and one-eighth to the advancement of religion.

Today, with charities having the immensely greater incomes we shall be examining, it is estimated that only about 27 per cent of the major ones exist for the relief of poverty and of sickness, ten per cent for the advancement of religion, and 29 per cent for general or multiple objects. Comment the Commissioners: "... charitable effort has largely moved away from its traditional objects of relief of poverty and sickness and advancing education into new areas."

The Commissioners cite as examples of the new areas, charities established to meet social needs arising from the changing organization and outlook of society. These include helping drug addicts, promoting family planning, general environmental aims, and the promotion of research, arts, culture and recreation. "Thus," say the Commissioners, "many charities now on the register exist for, or embrace, objects which differ greatly from the general idea of charity in 1876 or even 20 years ago. This is surely as it should be and it has been fortunate that the concept of charity in English law has been sufficiently flexible to allow this development to take place."

Under the heading 'Inquiries and investigations' the Commissioners deal, quite bluntly, with some of the things that worry the public about charities. They make very important observations and lay down guide-lines. The italics are mine.

> The inquiries we make in discharging our general function of promoting the effective use of charitable resources by the investigation and checking of abuses are in the main informal and undertaken with the willing co-operation of the trustees. The matters needing investigation have in general fallen into the following broad categories: technical breaches of trust where the trustees have misunderstood the purposes of their trusts and have in good faith acted outside them; inefficient and therefore misleading presentation of accounts; and projects which have been too ambitiously con-

ceived at the outset and have run into difficulties when public support has not come up to unrealistic expectations.

There is also the constantly recurring problem of administration costs, including fund-raising expenses, which are out of proportion to the amount of income actually made available for charitable purposes. It sometimes seems that fund-raising activities tend to become the be-all and end-all of a charity's existence. The true measure of a charity's effectiveness is not the amount of money it raises but the extent to which the money raised is used to achieve the objects set out in its trusts.

We have noticed a tendency for a few charities *of comparatively recent foundation* to give priority to establishing a well-equipped office in a good locality, with salaried staff suitable for a large well-established institution, the founders perhaps anticipating a success which they have not yet achieved rather than ensuring that from the outset the major portion of the money raised from the public is devoted to the charitable purpose for which appeals have been made.

It cannot be too strongly emphasized that fund-raising and efficient administration are means only to the carrying out of a trust's charitable purposes. If over a number of years the money raised by a charity is largely absorbed by administrative expenses or by the cost of further fund-raising and little is actually applied to the charitable purposes for which the charity exists, the question must arise whether the organization is really operating as a charity.

One principle which we sometimes find it necessary to emphasize in the course of our inquiries is that *a trustee must not make a profit from his trust and that this prevents him from making an arrangement whereby he receives a salary or commission from the trust funds.* Those who devote a large amount of their time to founding and running a charity in an honorary capacity may later on have to face the choice between retaining control of the charity and accepting the principle of non-payment for services rendered and of becoming a paid employee of the charity under the control of other and independent trustees.

2

ATTITUDES AND ANIMOSITIES

Whatever definitions one uses for charity, it is very questionable whether all giving is rooted in love; there are many professional charity officials who will say that two major factors are 'a pricking of the conscience' and 'keeping up with the Joneses'. Cynical they may be, but they know the field. They will tell you that the majority of people in Britain will do anything but give cash: they'll go to charity football matches or a dance, they'll buy raffle tickets, fill in pools coupons and they'll buy charity Christmas cards (because they are generally less expensive than ordinary commercial ones). But in terms of hard cash they give per head only about one-eighth of what American individuals do. That is why people complain about flag days or door-to-door collections, where someone stares them in the eye and rattles the box . . . it is difficult to get out of giving then. And charities know very well the value of using pretty girls for flag days! The professional fund-raisers operate in a similar way even though they scorn the penny collections and go instead for the big money. They use methods which, in effect, shame people into giving money: 'Sir Joseph has given us £1,000 and suggested I ask you . . .'. That sort of thing generally works.

Charitable funds have been established out of vanity, out of prejudice, out of spite. Whim plays its part also. There is, or was, a girl in Peterborough, Northants, who has accumulated 27 engagement rings. She is hoarding them all, and any more she may gather in, until the day she marries when, she says, "I'll give them all to charity!"

An invaluable piece of research into the British public's attitude to charity was carried out for the Royal National Institute for the Blind. This baldly recorded: "The prevalent attitude towards charities is one of hostility; this is not due to the aims of charity, which are generally acknowledged to be laudable, but to the fact that in the eyes of the public the main activity in which any charity is engaged with direct relation to them is the parting of the individual and his money."

The antagonism to flag days and door to door selling extends to an attitude of greater or lesser animosity to all charities and the guilt-feeling of people who think like this makes them more critical. Says the report:

> Most reasons for reluctance to contribute to charity are obvious rationalizations – 'It's the responsibility of the State' . . . 'There are plenty of people who enjoy doing it' – but there is one aspect which has the aura of a genuine grievance. This is the considerable suspicion displayed towards the expenditure of charities on administration costs, particularly in areas where several charities are involved in catering for the same group of people, as was the case with cancer research and is the case with charities for the blind. When a specific target is set for collection – in the form, for example, of a dormobile for taking crippled children camping – there is much less reluctance to contribute, probably because it is felt that one knows precisely what the money donated is being used for. This form of collection also provides the donor with a certain degree of self-satisfaction by enabling identification with a particular project rather than the anonymity of simply 'putting a shilling in the blind box'. The nineteenth-century concept of charities as an activity of the rich to help the poor is dying hard. The animosity towards administration costs is partly a reflection of this, since those who work for charities are still regarded primarily as volunteers who, if they are not wealthy in their own right, certainly have no right to live comfortably on a salary received from a charity. Oddly enough, however, this attitude does not extend to advertising, which appears to be accepted as a necessary part of a charity's activities. It is also possible that an advertisement for charity offers the possibility of taking no action and this does not arouse the hostility of the direct confrontation.

Again and again in their discussions with people the research company came up against voluble resentment of door-to-door collections and flag days, precisely because they were hard to turn down even though most people felt it right to help other people – 'even as a sop to the conscience' as some put it. Generally people seem to feel that ten pence is the right sum to give a collector – except in church, where they can get away with two pence – but many argue that if they gave ten pence to all charities they would be bankrupt! The researchers estimated that an average person gives a total of about £1.20 per year to charity, though other analysts think it is more, as will be seen later.

The report also showed up hostility to individual causes, especially charities concerned with overseas aid the 'Why should we send money out to natives' reaction. Animal charities produce a typically ambiguous attitude where Britons and animals are concerned. There is no great amount of resentment towards them but there is a feeling that someone who admitted to a reluctance to give for humans ought not to admit also to a soft spot for cats and dogs.

People get *bored* with appeals from established charities, continuing ones, and in this piece of research the blind were particularly mentioned, even though most people felt that blindness was the worst thing that could happen to them . . . but 'It never could happen to me!' Frequently there was the old argument that with the Welfare State charity-giving should be unnecessary, although some people conceded that charities provided the 'extras' that no Government would – 'Governments don't provide outings and holidays', or 'They'd survive in these homes but they wouldn't have any pleasures'.

Other attitudes that emerged in the report emphasized people's wish to shrug off responsibility on to someone else, anyone else. There were people who pointed out that charity benefited the donor as well as the recipient; it was 'good for the soul', provided it was somebody else's soul. Then there was the typical, all-too-revealing comment: 'There are so many people in the world very keen on helping anybody that's deprived.' And the next attitude, closely linked, was expressed thus: 'I think it would be dreadful if the State took over the lifeboats for instance. Everybody says this is a responsibility of the State but it would completely destroy the very basis of the thing, the basis that it's a voluntary organization. People do it because they want to, because they're connected with the sea.'

The strongest resentments against charity were expressed by people who were 'a little bit sickened by reports of the amount of charity money collected that goes to the administration process' and by the way in which – it was claimed – several charities work for the same end. As for charity officials being properly paid, this was deliciously reflected in the following quote from one woman which sums up a widespread attitude: 'I say just because a man is employed to raise money for charities there's no reason why he should live like a pauper. But my husband says no, but he needn't necessarily fly himself, his wife and three children to Majorca every year for a holiday, need he?'

The researchers in this operation recommended that it is better to appeal for limited aims and specific targets so that people could feel sure that the money went to a given purpose and could identify themselves with it. It was pointed out also that people who had some personal connection with a charity's aims showed more willingness to give of their time, but less markedly of their money, to a specific cause: a woman whose mother suffered from mental illness helped in the local hospital for such cases; a woman with a diabetic son held coffee mornings, and so on. One might wonder whether there is a 'keeping up with the Joneses' background to the reported case of the man who said he always gave to appeals for spina bifida babies . . . since one of his neighbours had started a nursery for them.

It was found that people didn't mind collecting old newspapers or milk bottle tops for specific causes, such as guide dogs for the blind, and there are some people who assert that the help is given here not so much for the blind as for the dog!

The same organization was commissioned by the R.N.I.B. to prepare an 'Awareness Study' to find out how well people distinguish one charity from another. The survey here was conducted with a random selection of 2,658 people across Britain. They were given a list of prominent charities and asked which ones they knew. The R.S.P.C.A. and N.S.P.C.C. came first (surprisingly one might think) with 98 per cent recognizing them; 97 per cent had heard of the Cancer Research Campaign and 96 per cent of the R.N.I.B. The Royal National Lifeboat Institute and Oxfam each scored 94 per cent and next, with 89 per cent, came the Save the Children Fund. The returns went down to 80 per cent for the Royal National Institute for the Deaf, to 71 per cent for Shelter, and 61 per cent for Help the Aged.

But a trick question had been included. In the list was one totally non-existent charity named 'Helping Hands', and no less than 32 per cent of the people questioned claimed to know it!

Analyzing the response according to socio-economic status, it was found that most charities were less known among the DE (or lowest) grade. It is suggested that this is because they read less. It was found that 89 per cent of ABs knew of Shelter, for example, but only 57 per cent of DEs. The R.N.I.B., R.S.P.C.A., N.S.P.C.C. and the Cancer Research Campaign were more or less equally well-known to all grades. In only one case was there a difference between men and women: 58 per cent of men had heard of Help the Aged but 64 per cent of women.

Touching on the question of the involvement of youth in charity today, it was found that Shelter and the Save the Children Fund were better known as the age group of those questioned became lower. Of the 16-24 age group, 77 per cent knew Shelter; in the over-65s the percentage fell to 59. Only one charity became better known with age – Help the Aged. There was a slight tendency for people in Scotland to be less aware of most charities than other areas, and awareness generally tended to be slightly higher in the south-east of England.

3

FROM WHENCE . . . AND TO WHERE?

Some of the most detailed investigations into charity giving have been made by Colonel Lewis G. Wells, the American-born founder of the Wells International Donors Advisory Services, a fund-raising and advisory company of which his son, Frank H. Wells, is chairman. In around 50 years of full-time professional fund-raising, Colonel Wells has pulled in a total of more than £1,000 million for almost every kind of charity in every major English-speaking country. His organization is the first to point to the notorious difficulty of securing accurate figures of charity giving and the dangers of comparisons between concerns with differing financial years.

The figures given here are necessarily only 'guestimates' and probably understate the position. However, in 1972 the Wells organization worked on a figure of 180,000 organizations that could be recognized as charities. These were the 1971 figure of 80,000 charities, trusts and foundations on the Charity Commissioner's Register for England and Wales, 25,000 then registered by the Department of Education and Science, 10,000 by the Northern Ireland Government, 15,000 in Scotland, and 50,000 churches. Wells estimated that in 1971 the total annual giving in the United Kingdom was about £250 million and listed what they frankly called 'arbitrary assumptions' as to where this came from. On these figures the pattern of giving in 1971 would be like this:

	Total giving	*For religion*	*For education, arts & research*	*For health & welfare*
Total giving	£250m	£125m	£50m	£75m
Individuals	£125m	£75m	£7.5m	£42.5m
Bequests	£50m	£20m	£10m	£20m
Companies	£30m	£2.5m	£20m	£7.5m
Foundations	£45m	£27.5m	£12.5m	£5m

Total American giving in 1971 was estimated at £8,812m, of which £6,292m came from individuals, £1,215m from bequests, £414m from companies, and £854m from foundations. Out of the total, £3,586m went to religion, £1,383m to education, arts and research, and £3,842m to health and welfare. American individual giving *per capita* was £30.69 for the year and British £2.27. If one takes *all* giving, it was about £43 *per capita* in the United States (2.1 per cent of the Gross National Product) and £4.54 in Britain (one-half per cent of the G.N.P.).

It is above all else difficult to produce anything like accurate statistics for religious giving, but it has been estimated that there are now some 58,000 churches or congregations in Britain, with a nominal total of about 40.8m men, women and children involved. It is thought that about £64m is given annually in offerings and that the total annual income of all related churches and charities may reach more than £125m. A breakdown of some actual and some estimated church statistics for Britain could look like this:

	Churches/ congregations	*Membership*	*Offerings*	*Total income from all sources*
Anglican & Presbyterian	20,000	28m	£26m	£67m
Roman Catholic	4,400	5m	£15m	£20m
Scottish & Presbyterian	3,850	3.3m	£11m	£14.5m
Methodist	10,500	2.2m	£6.2m	£7.75m
Congregational	4,000	420,000	£2m	£2.5m
Baptist	4,000	500,000	£1.6m	£2m
Jewish	–	450,000	–	£9m

Of all religious giving in Britain, it is estimated that about £75m comes annually from living individuals, £20m from bequests and legacies, £2.5m from companies, and £27.5m from charitable trusts, including £23m from the Church of England Commissioners. Religious giving in Britain rose by 3.6 per cent in a year to reach 50 per cent of all giving in 1971/72.

So far as church giving is concerned it is certain that the figures quoted are underestimates, if only because so many different charitable projects are carried on by all denominations that are not reflected in formal 'collection' figures –

coffee mornings and whist drives for instance. These activities are not confined to churches: other examples of informal fund-raising are the efforts in pubs and clubs, at sports functions, during darts matches and on similar occasions, all impossible to assess accurately. A typical publican calculates that he raises £500 a year for charitable purposes, mostly for the handicapped, by raffles across the bar. Others collect money for strictly local causes – the aged or a neighbourhood orphanage perhaps – and this money usually does not show up in national statistics or in the revenues of charity organizations. There are some 60,000 pubs in England and Wales and if only ten per cent of them raised £500 a year in this way the total would come to £3 million. Big as that is, it too is probably a conservative figure and does not include the large sums that licensed victuallers raise for their own charities.

Guesses or not, the Wells figures seem to be supported by extrapolating a British Government family expenditure survey in 1969 which reported that the average expenditure on charitable donations and subscriptions by the 7,008 households which co-operated in the survey was £5,356 p.a., excluding covenant refunds and membership subscriptions. This, on the basis of about 18,750,000 households in the United Kingdom then, would mean a total of £100,425,000, to which could be added some £15m for covenant refunds and about £10m for membership subscriptions, or about £125m in all. The survey indicated, by the way, that 58 per cent of all householders were non-givers to charity, or that more than half the 55.5m population of the United Kingdom do not support *any* voluntary religious, educational, health or welfare activities.

Now for some figures from the Government's Blue Book on National Income and Expenditure 1971. Between 1962 and 1971 total personal incomes almost doubled from £24,000m to £47,000m. In the same period wages and salaries paid by private non-profit making bodies – including charities – increased by 280 per cent from £203m to £477m. Grants to private non-profit making bodies tripled to reach £378m in 1971, while grants to research councils rose more than five-fold to £131m. Transfers to charities from companies rose from £21m in 1962 to £38m in 1971, not including covenant tax refunds. Total covenant tax refunds to charities in 1971 were £16m, which indicates that in that year about £41.2m was given under charitable covenants by both companies and individuals.

The Church of England Year Book 1971/72 records that the ordinary annual income of C. of E. parishes almost doubled from under £15m in 1958 to £29m in 1968.

During the decade up to 1971, giving generally in the United Kingdom probably about doubled, as it has done throughout the English-speaking world, and the income of many of the largest charities in Britain more than doubled, following closely on the rise in incomes. There is no reason in 1974 to suppose that the trend has slowed down. Just one rather spectacular example. Heading a list of the largest charities in the United Kingdom at the start of 1972 was the Joint Palestine Appeal, with an income for the year to September, 1971 of £8,246,000, compared with £5,048,000 in 1970, all raised by the United Kingdom's Jewish population of 450,000 for charitable relief work in Israel. The Joint Palestine Appeal, which is a central collecting agency for a number of registered Jewish charities, such as the Society of Friends of Jewish Refugees, must be the only charity organization in Britain operating under constant guard! Its offices in London's Haymarket are over a BBC studio and . . . Iraqui Airlines. Bodyguards accompany all visitors to J.P.A. officials and the staff have to escort the visitors out of the building. Administration costs of raising that £8.245m worked out at between five and six per cent.

Here is a list of the top 20 fund-raising charities in the United Kingdom as they stood at the beginning of 1972, placed in order of the amount raised during a year. The figures cover varying financial year-endings, ranging from March to December 1971.

Organization	*Total gross income*	*% of previous year*	*Gifts, legacies*	*Legacies only*	*Rents & investment income*	*Assets*
	000s	*000s*	*000s*	*000s*	*000s*	*000s*
Joint Palestine Appeal	£8,246	163	£8,246	–	–	£230
Dr Barnardo's Homes	£4,345	114	£2,874	£1,641	£523	£11,745
Christian Aid	£2,907	111	£2,719	£70	£68	£421
Imperial Cancer Research Fund	£4,076	144	£2,717	£1,895	£1,359	£13,258
Oxfam	£3,301	99	£2,670	£277	£33	£715
Cancer Research Campaign	£2,873	103	£2,490	£1,214	£384	£5,698
Royal National Lifeboat Institution	£2,613	108	£2,445	£1,062	£168	£3,817

Organization	*Total gross income*	*% of previous year*	*Gifts, legacies*	*Legacies only*	*Rents & investment income*	*Assets*
Spastics Society	£2,940	99	£2,433	£369	£507	£10,412
Save the Children Fund	£3,111	133	£2,388	£74	£86	£1,508
Royal British Legion	£1,979	112	£1,728	£76	£178	£3,229
Royal National Institute for the Blind	£3,124	103	£1,678	£911	£141	£3,878
Royal Society for the Prevention of Cruelty to Animals	£1,538	66	£1,659	£1,413	£466	£5,627
Church of England Children's Society	£1,914	106	£1,457	£558	£149	£2,656
Church Missionary Society	£1,545	103	£1,404	£531	£80	£985
National Society for the Prevention of Cruelty to Children	£1,539	119	£1,389	£445	£126	£2,654
Methodist Missionary Society	£1,781	103	£1,351	£158	£49	£5,480
Help the Aged	£1,151	133	£1,151	—	—	£229
National Children's Homes	£1,557	115	£1,107	£293	£83	£7,376
National Trust	£3,360	123	£1,106	£556	£1,515	£15,803
St Dunstan's	£1,705	104	£961	£946	£744	£16,573

Many interesting points emerge from this list. When we consider the assets of the various organizations it can be seen that St Dunstan's is the wealthiest. The National Trust is in a unique position since its work is concerned with valuable property and it is not comparable with any other charity. Dr Barnardo's, for one, runs homes which have to be valued in the books. In fact asset figures can be highly misleading. All the charities listed here ended the year better off, with the exception of Oxfam, the Spastics Society, and the Royal Society for the Prevention of Cruelty to Animals. The enormous proportion of the R.S.P.C.A.'s income that comes from legacies alone may be noticed; also the fact that the

British public gave £270,000 more to the animal organization than to the children's one. However, more about this point later.

On the other hand the Save the Children Fund increased its assets by no less than 33 per cent, as did the then relatively new Help the Aged, an organization which had as yet no help from rents or investments and little from legacies.

The 'Top Twenty' received slightly more than £44m in gifts and legacies in the year; the leading fifty just under £60m, and the first hundred £65.5m. Revenues from gifts and legacies of some of the smaller but well-known charities during the year included: Shelter £865,000 (a fall of 11 per cent on the previous year), the Cheshire Homes £756,000, British and Foreign Bible Society £754,000, Marie Curie Memorial Foundation £714,000, National Society for Cancer Relief £703,000, the R.A.F. Benevolent Fund £563,000, the Scouts £291,000, Red Cross £290,000, the Salvation Army (with assets of £6,377,000) £254,000, the Royal National Institute for the Deaf £205,000 – compared with £210,000 raised in the Greater London area alone for the blind – and Alexandra Day £169,000. Blue Cross got £199,000 for animals and the Young Men's Christian Association came next with £197,000. The Young Women's Christian Association, however, could raise only £67,000.

One area where it *is* possible to get closer to reasonably accurate figures of charity giving is the very important field of Big Business, which in the United Kingdom annually donates about one-quarter of one per cent of its pre-tax profits. The Wells organization says that all the United Kingdom companies in the private sector, and employing 18,300,000 people, gave about £30m to charity in 1971. Of this total, £2.5m was for religious purposes, £10m for the arts, education and research and £20m for health and welfare.

The hundred most generous United Kingdom companies gave £8,329,638, a rise of three per cent on the previous year, and one half of one per cent of their post-tax profits, which rose in total by 16 per cent in the year. Very broadly, the more profitable the company, the more is given to charity, though there were quite a number of companies which made larger profits than some of the top 20 givers and yet gave less.

The following list of the 20 most generous companies shows the amount they gave, the rise or fall on the 1970 figure, in nearly all cases the 1971 profit after tax, and the rise or fall in profit on 1970.

Company	*1971 giving*	*% of 1970*	*1971 profit*	*% of 1970*
Wellcome Foundation	£2,126,285	101	£4,408,000	101
Imperial Chemical Industries	£431,000	90	£85,300,000	93
Shell Petroleum	£312,000	102	£108,877,000	121
Unilever	£304,000	129	£38,200,000	131
British Petroleum	£269,678	131	£81,900,000	105
Marks & Spencer	£197,000	111	£31,215,000	120
Barclays Group	£165,167	107	£46,705,000	128
Courtaulds	£132,000	117	£23,775,000	89
Boots	£131,000	*452	£14,222,000	129
Imperial Tobacco	£120,167	110	£43,974,000	111
General Electric	£120,000	104	£36,001,000	120
I.B.M.	£112,000	170	£25,049,000	92
National Westminster Bank	£106,002	87	£48,666,000	129
Midland Bank	£101,000	100	£30,485,000	118
Esso Petroleum	£98,092	95	£9,234,000	—
Rio Tinto-Zinc	£97,000	109	£19,000,000	70
Lloyds Bank	£91,000	103	£33,787,000	141
Rank Organization	£90,771	84	£21,540,000	111
Ford Motor	£87,000	70	£17,500,000	—
Philips Electronic	£84,000	100	—	—

* Includes £100,000 endowment.

Twenty-first in the list is the B.A.T. Group with £82,955, a 40 per cent rise on the previous year's giving. The other tobacco companies listed are Carreras, 47th with £44,208, and Gallaher, 58th, with £37,766. The liquor companies listed are Guinness, 28th, with £65,920, Distillers, 39th (£54,000), Whitbreads 41st (£52,376), Bass Charington 53rd (£39,080), Allied Breweries 54th (£39,056), Watney Mann 73rd (£28,373), and Courage 77th (£25,880). All the liquor companies except Guinness gave a few per cent less than the previous year, although 1971 profit increases ranged from 14 to 32 per cent up on 1970. Guinness, with a profit rise of 24 per cent, gave an additional one per cent. Gifts from the big insurance companies ranged from £41,005 from the Prudential, 50th on the list, to £16,700 from Royal Insurance, who were 96th. Vickers, with profits up 60 per cent on 1970, cut donations by 52 per cent to £29,887, while the Bank of Scotland with profits up 29 per cent, cut back 51 per cent to £18,474. The Bank of England was 27th on the list with donations of £68,797, or 25 per cent more than in 1970, though profits in 1971 dropped by 14 per cent.

None of the figures in the list includes donations outside

the United Kingdom. The financial years involved ended at various times between March 1971 and February 1972.

Apart from receiving financial support from the government – which came to about £171.5m in 1971 – Britain's 50 universities benefit from charity, and Wells calculates that they received some £6m in gifts and legacies during the year. The total estimated annual giving for all educational purposes in the United Kingdom for 1971/72 is £50m, of which £7.5m came from living individuals, £10m from bequests and legacies, £20m from companies, and £12.5m from charitable trusts. The United Kingdom gave 91p *per capita* to education in the year, the United States £6.75m.

The assets of the 50 universities for 1971 were estimated at £1,107m, with an aggregate income for the year from all sources of £313m. As far as can be determined the biggest income from gifts and legacies was received by Stirling University (£374,000), followed by Surrey (£340,000), Cambridge (£280,000), Strathclyde (£215,000), Oxford (£166,000) and Sussex (£162,000).

The charity umbrella can also be extended to cover a number of voluntary membership, charitable or non-profit making organizations, such as certain professional societies and institutions like the Royal College of Nursing, Royal Society of Medicine and others. In 1971 the 50 largest such professional organizations had a total income of £13,750,000 which was an increase of 14 per cent on the previous year. Receipts from gifts and legacies are not known precisely but here are some 1971 figures for the largest five organizations by membership.

Organization	*Members 000s*	*Membership fees 000s*	*Total income 000s*	*% of previous year*
Institution of Professional Civil Servants (Non-profit)	90	£378	£447	118
Institute of Bankers (Non-profit)	86	£157	£376	106
Royal College of Nursing (Charity)	82	£204	£528	121

Organization	*Members 000s*	*Membership fees 000s*	*Total income 000s*	*%of previous year*
Institution of Mechanical Engineers (Non-profit)	73	£446	£501	101
Institution of Electrical Engineers (Non-profit)	64	£298	£550	101

C.B.D. Research Ltd, who publish a directory of more than 6,000 British associations, have estimated that a complete directory for voluntary organizations in the British Isles would contain well over a quarter of a million entrics without including friendly societies, building societies, benevolent societies, trade unions, churches and religious groups. These voluntary non-profit making associations include, for example, motoring, sporting and cultural associations of many kinds. There are in addition more than 1,000 governmental or semi-governmental councils and committees, such as the Science Research Council, Arts Council and Sports Council. As already mentioned, Government grants to non-profit making bodies and research councils in 1971 came to £509m, which may really be added to the total charitable giving in the United Kingdom for that year.

4

THE BIG TRUSTS

Although millions of pounds a year are given directly to charity in its widest sense by Britain's charitable trusts, or foundations, *their* revenue has not been included in my figure of £300m donated in 1973 to charity. With a few exceptions, the major foundations never receive gifts or legacies from the public; their annual revenues come from investments and these, of course, will vary according to the financial condition of their shares from time to time.

To that £300m figure it is probably reasonable to add £65m received by foundations from all sources. In 1972 Wells listed the 50 largest foundations in the United Kingdom, excluding fund-raising charities, Government-funded agencies and certain organizations with large assets, such as housing trusts and benevolent associations. Many of the figures available refer to different financial years. With this qualification, he gave the listed foundations a total annual income then of £54m and reported aggregate assets of no less than £712.7m. It is almost certain that these assets are considerably higher in 1974. These 50 pay out about £38m a year in grants in the United Kingdom.

Heading this league then – and it will still do so today – were the Church Commissioners, with an annual income of around £25.4m. There followed the Gulbenkian Foundation which is based in Portugal but makes very substantial grants to British organizations and causes each year from its income of about £10m annually. Among the largest British private foundations are: Nuffield, Wolfson, Wellcome, Rank, Leverhulme, Rowntree, Hayward, and King Edward's Hospital Fund. Other important and famous ones include the Garfield Weston Foundation, King George's Jubilee Trust, the Pilgrim Trust, Carnegie Trust, Winston Churchill Memorial Trust, Cadbury, the Bernard Sunley Charitable Foundation, and the three Clore family trusts with an annual income at the time the list was compiled of £129,000, making them joint 33rd on the Wells list.

These family trusts are particularly interesting, carrying on as they do the rich nobles' ancient tradition of charity, now taken over by the leaders of industry and trade. There are no less than eleven formed by the Cadburys between 1920 and 1948 (total yearly income around £207,000), four Marks (£109,000), eleven Rank, formed between 1918 and 1970 (£1,173,000), and six Wolfson, formed between 1955 and 1961 (£2,665,000).

What sort of activities do the foundations engage in? Above everything else, it can be said that they are pace-makers for the State. A number of the big foundations have been created during the past 50 years; their objects are far-ranging and, since most of them distribute only the income of the foundation, they can make long-term, durable plans for aid. Such trusts give special assistance to pioneer and experimental work, tending each to select their own favourite field. Generally they help the cause or project involved until it is firmly established and the burden of support is taken up either by the State or by the public. Many of these trusts are generous supporters of the arts, sciences and medicine. The foundations have one supreme advantage, low costs of administration, because unlike the fund-raising charities they have usually got their money already and do not have to spend on advertising, promotions or collecting. This makes an enormous difference to their effectiveness pound for pound of revenue.

The Nuffield Foundation (assets more than £20m) draws its income largely from the £10m worth of Morris Motor shares given by Lord Nuffield in 1943. With a staff of 30, running costs are eight per cent of income. The Nuffield provides research grants to universities, gives donations to arts centres, and was, for instance, responsible for a £1.5m research programme into education and examinations that led directly to the establishment of the Schools Council and important changes in the way subjects are treated in schools. Nuffield takes particular care to not leave its projects open to a sudden cut-off or reduction in funds. If it decides to make a grant of £5,000 a year for five years, say, the whole £25,000 involved is set aside at the start. The trust gets around ten applications *a day* for grants to help a wide spectrum of projects and aims. They gave £30,000 towards the cost of research into pollution in the Lower Swansea Valley, in which the Government and the local authority eventually joined. They supported four years' research, conducted by Dr Hilde Himmelweit, into the effect of television on children and that in due course led to studies by the BBC and ITV. It pioneered research into race relations and has now set aside £150,000 to examine the best ways of providing legal aid and advice to those who cannot go and get it for themselves.

The Wolfson family established their foundation in 1955 with £6m, largely in shares in Great Universal Stores, and the foundation is now worth about £40m. Wolfson also gets about ten applications for aid daily, sometimes as many as 15. Their broad terms of reference are the advancement of education and health in the United Kingdom and Commonwealth. To these ends Wolfson especially provides money for buildings: a Cambridge Institute of Theoretical Astronomy, new premises for the Royal College of Physicians, the Hunterian Museum of the Royal College of Surgeons, new libraries for the Royal College of Music and for the Royal Society, and so on. They also gave £80,000 to extend a hospice for patients dying of cancer. The Wolfson trustees – three members of the family, a scientist, two medical men, two historians and a judge – must be unanimous in their decision to give or not to give to a particular cause. Of recent years they have extended their support to research projects linked to industry and which might improve the British economy. Here the mentality of the businessman is seen! If a university, for instance, gets a Wolfson grant for the development of an invention and profits start to flow from the patent rights, the university is expected to repay the money, or part of it, to help finance further grants.

The public does give money to King Edward's Hospital Fund for London, founded in 1897 by King Edward VII when he was Prince of Wales to mark Queen Victoria's diamond jubilee. Among *single* gifts have been sums like £1.3m, £526,000, £483,000 and £420,000 and today the fund's assets stand around £16m, with an income of almost £750,000 in 1971. Where does the money go since the National Health Service came into being? Very much the question that people ask. Well, the fund helps about 200 hospitals and homes in London *which lie outside the N.H.S.* and in N.H.S. hospitals it provides amenities which the State cannot or will not afford. Some years ago they set a precedent by establishing post-graduate medical centres in some hospitals – today these are an accepted feature of hospital organization. With the prime aim of improving the care obtainable in hospitals, the fund has a College of Hospital Management, providing, among others, courses for administrative, medical, nursing and catering staff. The fund started the Emergency Bed service, which finds beds for general practitioners' patients, and is now supporting services for the medically handicapped, care of the elderly, and integration of health services generally. With Lambeth Council, St Thomas's Hospital and the City Parochial Foundation, they built a holiday home by the sea for severely physically handicapped people.

The City Parochial Foundation had assets at March, 1970 of around £2.8m and an annual income of some £368,000. This foundation was established by Parliament in 1883 to administer the individual charities of all the City of London C. of E. parishes except the five largest. Later it took in the Metropolitan Police area. Today the foundation's assets have been reported at perhaps £10m and its annual income around £600,000. About a third of the income goes to the Church Commissioners, who attend to the repair of churches. The balance goes in grants to organizations helping the poor. "We try to point the way to the Government of how things might be done", they say. They establish things like mother and baby centres, children's clubs and housing advice centres, and often these eventually draw the support of the local authority or the Government once they have been launched and seen to work!

When he died in 1925, Lord Leverhulme created his foundation with shares in the Unilever company. Income from these shares has risen from £15,000 in 1925 to more than a million a year today and in 1970 they paid out £627,000 in grants within the United Kingdom. Most of this goes to projects in education and research, about 70 per cent of them people or organizations that just apply out of the blue. They have a research awards advisory committee which dispenses fellowships and grants worth about £600,000 annually. These, for example, enable people to write books on an extraordinary range of subjects, some which might otherwise never seen the light of day. They prefer to aid projects and activities for which public money is not easily available and sometimes take on research at the request of the Government when it isn't prepared to pay itself! Among recent major grants have been £75,000 for a study of productivity bargaining and the redeployment of labour, and £81,000 for a study of women and careers.

Yet another pace-setter is the Pilgrim Trust, established in 1930 with £2m given by an American named Edward Harkness, whose family had lived in Dumfriesshire in 1716. With investments worth more than £8m, its yearly income is around £350,000. The original aims of the foundation were the 'preservation of the national heritage and the future well-being of the country'. About 120 separate grants are made annually for the preservation of buildings and the countryside, for art and learning, and for social welfare. In 1939 the Pilgrim Trust started C.E.M.A., the Council for the Encouragement of Music and the Arts, which the State took over in 1945 and re-named the Arts Council. The trust helps legal aid centres, handicapped and delinquent children, and polio victims. It gave £50,000 towards the fund to keep Titian's *Death of Actaeon* in Britain.

Bernard Sunley started in business as a small builder and died a millionaire in 1964. The grants made by the Bernard Sunley Charitable Foundation reflect the man who set it up. With assets, at 1971 values, of £1.1m and an annual income then of £250,000, it paid out £343,000 in grants that year. Typical recipients since 1964 have been a sports centre at Gordonstoun, the National Army Museum, the Hertford British Hospital in Paris, and St Paul's Cathedral. It is now establishing a £250,000 home for old people.

Frequently the administrators of these foundations are asked – as are their opposite numbers in fund-raising charities – if the work could not be done better by a small number of central funds or even a single immense charity which would dispense money according to its assessment of need. The inquirers have in mind something like the American Community Chest system, which has simply not caught on in Britain.

In the United States and Canada people have been trained to give to local organizations, sometimes called United Funds, from which money is allocated to various causes. Appeals for these 'Chests' are strictly limited to short periods and all charities seeking to raise money in the area must participate, they may not compete with the central fund on their own, 'selfish' account. The 'Chests' are consequently very large affairs, highly professionally managed on behalf of an organization of the *donors* – a 'Chest' is not an organization of the receivers. Under this system, as the North American sees it, the businessman can satisfy his charitable instincts once and for all on one brief exercise each year, rather than taking time out regularly to help four, five or six individual charities. Chest officers may not be representatives of recipients, indeed one American description of the Community Chest system called it 'a businessman's protection association'. Possibly for this reason the administration of a Community Chest is one of the highest-paying management jobs in the United States and Canada.

Under the Community Chest system the organizers must meet all recurring annual expenses of all the charities involved in their operation and may not accept gifts for investment or distribution in later years. The whole idea is to compress a massive and extremely intensive drive to collect all the money required into a short period – a week or at most a month.

With these limitations and rules, little of the system appeals in Britain for sundry reasons. The Nathan Committee on Charitable Trusts, set up by the Government, reported strongly in favour of some version of what are here called Common Good Funds, on both national and local levels. The Government rejected the national level suggestion but thought it might be advantageous if Common Good Funds were established more widely locally. It was considered for example that such funds could help co-ordinate the work of local charities and even take over the assets of charities no longer serving a useful purpose. Under the Charities Act of 1960 the term 'Common Good' may only be used with the permission of the Charity Commissioners. There have been very, very few attempts to form such funds although (see Chapter 9) there have been many amalgamations of charities in various areas. Despite St Paul's assertion, charity is a very jealous and prideful business! The big foundations and fund-raising charities, the tiny and ancient charities alike, are all united in one respect: they do not like amalgamations – indeed they positively fear them. Charity, they say with considerable truth, is a most personal affair; people give to what they know and like and will not support a vast amorphous body.

The late Lord Rosenheim, who was president of the Royal College of Physicians and one of the Wolfson trustees, was asked by Denis Hart, who wrote a study of the big foundations for the *Daily Telegraph Magazine*, if the charity money available in Britain would be more efficiently spent by one central body. Replied Lord Rosenheim:

> I would disagree . . . There is something personal about these foundations or trusts. A man can indulge his interests through his trust and he can be approached by his friends. A de-personalized charity wouldn't be the same. Frankly, I don't think the individual charitable millionaires would be much interested in it. They might as well give their money to the Government. The small sums that a

> foundation may give are often a seed and an encouragement. The fact that it gives £1,000 to something that's asking for £20,000 or £30,000 may be enough to put an appeal on its feet and get it going. If there was a central body pre-occupied with large projects, this wouldn't happen.

What holds good for the foundations' attitude to giving is true also of the individual donor. He wants to give his 10p, or leave his £50 legacy, to a favourite cause. He can be induced by example, conscience or direct personal appeal to give to other charities on occasion – unless he actively dislikes their aims – but the personal element comes into it every time.

5

PATTERNS OF CHANGE

"The poor you shall always have with you", said Jesus. Poverty is a very relative thing; when one person says "I'm poor" he may be regarded as living in positive luxury by the even less fortunate. While there can be said to be little *absolute* poverty and hunger in Britain today, the very advent of the Welfare State created an even greater need for private charity because it raised the standards of demand while still leaving so much undone. In the first place the State only does what it *must* when it is forced to it, and that generally only after private charity has first shown the way. All social growth in all countries has stemmed first from voluntary action. There are still enormous shortcomings in the National Health Service which can only be assuaged by private charitable work and money – for instance the provision of extra comforts in old people's homes and in geriatric wards, of swimming pools, gymnasia, libraries, films and TV sets for orphanages and the like. This has led directly to constant pressure on charities to raise ever more money year by year to meet modern demands. Today's people have been trained by the Welfare State to expect more as of right. Admittedly there are people who are too proud to go to the State for help, many who still do not know how to go about it anyway, yet they will generally accept private charity. One social worker had an elderly man, recently retired and living like a recluse on a tiny pension, who flatly refused to go to the local Social Security office, where he could have been helped. It emerged that he was too ashamed of his shabby clothes to be seen in the streets. Provided with clothes by a charitable fund, he was a new person. There are also people who have no compunction about extracting anything and everything they can from a charity. Said the same social worker: "Once when we went to a poor home we would have to persuade them to accept help of any kind. Today you are liable to be presented with a veritable 'shopping list' of real or imagined needs!" Charity organizers point also to the well-known fact that people give more willingly if it is a voluntary appeal. They certainly object to giving to the State, and one blanches to think what State taxation would amount to if all the functions of private charity were taken over.

Over the last 50 or 60 years there have been two social changes that have vitally affected charity giving and working. Once, inheriting the tradition of the monasteries, charitable work was predominantly sponsored by Church of England vicarages and the squirearchy, both much better-off then than they are today. There were also still enough of the really wealthy who, for whatever reasons, were able and willing to give. The wives of the wealthy and middle classes had domestic servants to free them for charitable work; their daughters were, by and large, never trained to go out to work and had plenty of time for knitting, sewing, helping in hospitals and homes, and there were thus a substantial and dedicated army of voluntary workers. Today the wealthy are few and far between, domestic servants even more rare, and daughters and something like 40 per cent of all wives free to do so, go out to work. As a result far fewer people have the time for voluntary work, at least until they retire, and then they may not always be at their most effective mentally and physically. This steady erosion of voluntary aid has meant that charities have been well on the way to losing the one advantage they had over profit-making organizations. Many of the old sources of voluntary help simply dried up with social change though, as we shall see, others are emerging.

The effects of high taxation, death duties, 'freeze' and 'squeeze', 'incomes policies' and inflation generally are all too well known to everybody and of course they have the same impact on charities. Times of economic stress limit the helpers just when the need for aid increases. Critics complain of the greater tendency of some charities to employ professional, full-time, paid workers (the pros and cons of this are discussed elsewhere in this book), but some of the factors operating on charity work are not obvious to the public. Britain's population is rising, and this means there are more people to be cared for one way or another sooner or later. The advances in medicine mean that people are living longer and the geriatric problem is already massive indeed. Modern stress and strain is blamed for the increase in mental illness. Of an average 445,000 hospital beds available in England and Wales at any one time, no less than 126,000 are reserved for mental patients. Expressed another way, out of the 9.2 hospital beds available daily per thousand of the population, 2.6 are for the mentally ill. To take another example of social change increasing the demand on charity, mongol children now live on to adulthood whereas in the past they generally died around the age of ten.

All these very real factors are but part of the picture. One of Britain's most eminent charity organizers made this point:

> In Victorian days charitable workers felt they were doing very well indeed if they gave bread and soup to the poor. Just imagine trying to get away with that today! Once a penny loaf salved many a conscience, now charity workers think bigger in every way. They themselves have been brought up to better things; given the chance they will now hand out cakes as well! Sometimes they go too far – it is little use bringing people up to a higher standard than they can sustain themselves. Once I heard of a charity organizer who was quite severely criticized by some of his co-workers because in converting a big house into a home for boys, he had the ballroom divided up into small cubicles in dormitory-style. 'Why not give the boys bedrooms of their own?' he was asked. He replied that most of the young boys for whom the home was intended had never had bedrooms of their own and probably would be scared to sleep alone.

There have been other changes. Support for many allegations that politics have entered too much into certain aspects of voluntary social work – that there is too much 'left-wing' bias – may be found in a report published early in 1974 by the Apex Charitable Trust, the Government-backed employment agency for ex-prisoners, which said flatly that many of the problems faced by ex-prisoners trying to find a new job after their release could be solved if social workers did not let their political prejudices stand in the way. Apex added that many social workers would not accept offers of help from multi-national companies of which they disapproved or from companies which traded with certain countries they did not favour. One social worker was quoted as saying that even if he were offered 20 houses by 'a property speculator', he would refuse them.

Said Apex: "A new breed of social worker has entered the field. They are the first to object if their clients are divided into those worthy or unworthy of help, yet they are prepared to divide donors in that way. They are quite happy to deny their clients the help which is available from these sources. It is the client who suffers."

Apex director Mr Freddie Pentney accused some social workers of being prepared to break laws they considered unworkable or unjust, including drug laws and the Industrial Relations Act, adding that when they feed such views to the people they are supposed to help, the result could be disastrous, even providing an excuse to offer violence to people the ex-prisoner did not like or to steal from them.

Apart from ever-rising calls on charity, the cost of their administration also rises continually. Many charities, especially those running orphanages, homes, hospitals and the like, have to pay for the professional services of doctors, nurses, matrons and teachers, who have to receive the agreed trade union or national scale for the job. Then again, while there is still a number of people who are prepared to work for charity in offices and in the field for a smaller salary than they would get from a commercial or professional job, the number who can afford to do so decreases every year.

Despite such problems, as we have seen, charity incomes mostly increase each year. The money comes from four main sources (1) grants from public funds, (2) income from investments, (3) grants from the charitable trusts, and (4) subscriptions, donations, legacies and bequests. The grants from public funds have increased as more and more charitable initiatives have attracted State support. Income from investments is often the main standby of some of the older charities. During the nineteenth century, in particular, people had a great respect for 'capital'; they left money to charities on condition that it was invested, the capital left untouched, and only the income was spent. People in those days were also more keen than at present for their names to be immortalized in the name of a charitable trust. Some of the older charities draw large incomes from investments but the trend is dying out and the investment income of such charities depends to a large extent on their past legacies. People today do not generally have the money to bequeath big sums and with the level of death duties now prevailing, this source is likely to diminish even further. The charitable trusts have largely taken over the role of the big individual donor. These trusts, some of which have been surveyed in the last chapter, provide about a sixth of the money given to charity in England and Wales.

For the majority of charities by far the largest source of revenue is individual donations, collections and so on. The money here still comes mostly from the middle income groups, who preserve some tradition of giving even if they can find less time for working on behalf of charity. It is the 'working classes' who are providing a rising proportion of voluntary help today. Says a prominent charity administrator:

> I think charities – at least some of them – are getting more and more left wing; they are moving away in control, in administration, from those people who are perfectly willing to serve on committees, lend their names and so on, always providing that this is secondary to their main interests: hunting, shooting and fishing! The move to the left; the greater appeal to the left makes sense because now the working classes, who are more likely to be left-wing, are just beginning to take up the ideals of philanthropy. In the past they were the receivers and, except in pennies at a time, never the givers. Now they have the money to give if they want to. But most of them still don't give their own cash, they are more likely to donate their time.

This is most marked with today's youth. More and more charities are finding that young people are willing to help, not only by collecting, but by part-time work of all kinds. It is true that, having as yet no domestic responsibilities like a wife, children and mortgage, they can afford to do so. They tend to help the charities they regard as most in need – charities for the aged, spastics, handicapped children, and the homeless. Their elders may criticize the boys' beards, long hair and sometimes strange garb, the girls' bedraggled looks and often even stranger garb, but one can see the critics shamed into giving cash by the youngsters who go round pubs, for instance, imperiously rattling their collection boxes. The young are forceful, brash maybe, but they get results in terms of money. Many of them have no time at all for what they call the 'war charities'. They say these mean nothing to them, and in some cases there is positive hostility towards certain funds.

Schools of all kinds do an enormous amount of work for charity nowadays and it is probably true to say that the greatest amount of help comes from comprehensive and secondary schools rather than grammar and private schools, though there are some notable exceptions. Here again, it is often more a matter of giving time than actual cash, though plenty of money is raised. School 'task forces' and charitable projects play an increasingly important role for charities with an appeal for youth.

6

'DOCTORS' AND 'DETECTIVES'

The ruling body for charities in England and Wales is the Charity Commissioners, three men with some of the powers of High Court judges, who combine the roles of advisers, inspectors, and sometimes detectives, though they would rather be referred to as 'doctors'. These are the men who oversee the thousands of charities, the vast majority small, but about 15,000 of them major 'national' organizations.

It was in 1853 that the Commissioners were established. For years there had been concern at the number of cases concerning charities piled up in the Court of Chancery – it could and often did take years to secure settlement, while the huge costs involved often swallowed the entire assets of a charity which had gone to, or been taken to, court. It was commonly said that once a charity got into Chancery it *never* got out – the lawyers got the charity!

By 1860 the Commissioners were making schemes for the regulation of charities, but for 100 years their powers covered only 'endowed' organizations and did not embrace fund-raising charities. Although the Commissioners are, strictly speaking, Civil Servants and come under the aegis of the Home Secretary, he has no power over them and, until 1960, they were appointed to hold office at the Queen's pleasure, like judges.

The Commissioners have a total staff of about 300, of which 100 run a branch office in Liverpool. Quite a number of the staff are lawyers but only two men are generally needed to be kept on what might be termed the 'detective' work (checking any suspected shady activities for example) and this reflects the general integrity of British charities as a whole. The Commissioners do investigate complaints from the public but they say that for every 200 complaints they get, probably only one will be valid.

Basically the Charity Commissioners exist to see that charity administrators adhere to their trusts, to the purpose for which their organization was set up, and for nothing else.

The Commissioners have the power to investigate administration, the executive committee, or the controlling committee of a charity, and to go over its accounts, but they may not interfere with the proper discretion of the trustees and attempt to run the charity for them. If anything is found to be radically wrong the Commissioners seek to persuade the trustees to put it right. Above all the Commissioners are concerned to see that a charity's funds are properly used for the purpose originally intended or, if that proves to be no longer possible, to reorganize matters so that the money can be spent on aims as near as possible to the original intention. And, although they have no authority in the matter, the Commissioners were partly responsible for the formation of a chain of agents in underdeveloped countries who investigate and make sure that money raised in Britain for charitable purposes abroad is in fact devoted to the proper purpose – something which has long been the subject of public scepticism and doubt.

Every charity which has an endowment, that is when the charity may only spend the income and not the capital, or income from an endowment must send in accounts to the Charity Commissioners who, though they do not say so themselves, play a considerable role in the prevention or cure of plain stupidity. Not everyone understands the complexities of the Stock Exchange, not everyone can handle investments wisely and buy or sell at the right time. A large number of charities, though it is decreasing, are administered by committees of what the charity 'professionals' call 'do-gooders' – elderly ladies and retired gentlemen. Not many people have the time to help charities until they do retire and as a rule people who have *just* retired from business or the Services make admirable administrators for a time. But they do tend to hang on and on! The times overtake them and they get out of their depth. This is where the Commissioners and their Official Charity Custodian can usefully come in.

The Charities Act of 1960, which tidied up much in the field, established the Official Custodian, who is a senior member of the Commission. He holds property in trust for charities although he has no power to play any role in the management of a charity's property. His services are free and his two main roles are the safe-keeping of securities entrusted to him and the remission of the income to charity trustees without deduction of income tax. At 31 December 1972 the Official Custodian held almost £163 million in sterling securities on behalf of charities. During that year cash turn-over reached a new peak of £88m. The Custodian accepts trusteeship of an average 500 charities a year.

In addition the Commissioners operate the Charities Official Investment Fund, in which any charity may invest its entire assets. This is a unit trust set up in 1963 which now has more than £62m in investments. Until 1961 trustees of a charity or a private trust were restricted by law almost entirely to investment in Government stocks and certain other first-class securities providing a fixed income and having a fixed redemption value. This was to avoid or at least reduce the risk of loss of capital and income through speculative investment, but inflation made so many inroads into the real value of capital and income that the true worth of many charity resources fell drastically. Under the Trustee Investments Act 1961, trustees may invest up to half of their property in a wide range of industrial and commercial ordinary shares but many charities have too small an income to invest in many different enterprises and so spread the risk. For this reason the Commissioners established their unit trust.

The Commissioners are constantly urging charities, especially small ones, to take advantage of the Official Investment Fund but all too many still exist, on a remorselessly declining scale, on fixed-interest, undated stock. Charity trustees can die without leaving adequate information and records and the capital just gets lost! With the unit trust this cannot happen.

The 1960 Charities Act radically revised the statutory basis of charity administration, strengthened the powers of the Commissioners in dealing with abuses, and instituted the Commissioners' unique register of charities. Entry on this register establishes for all legal purposes the charitable status of an organization. Most religious charities need not register because the various denominational bodies concerned already maintain permanent records which are accessible to the public. Among the exemptions are places of religious worship, including vestries and caretakers' houses; working funds – generally obtained from collections – which if invested would not produce an income of more than £100 a year; charities for the maintenance of tombs and so on with an income of less than £15 a year.

An important point that is not always understood is that the fact that the Commissioners accept a charity on the register does not necessarily mean that they approve of it, of its officers, or of its methods of operation. In fact, anyone can set up a charity, saint or sinner, and the Commissioners have no power to bar him on grounds of character alone. There is one case of a man with several convictions for sexual assaults who established a fund to provide hostels . . . for teenage girls!

The Commissioners must satisfy themselves that an applying organization is in fact a charity in law and the difficulty of doing this is sometimes made greater by the fact that there is no statutary definition of 'charity'. The point was raised in Parliament during the debates on the Charities Bill, but it was agreed that it was impossible to draft anything that would be satisfactory. When approached by a new charity requesting registration, the Commissioners do not always find it possible – and nor is it strictly part of their duties – to satisfy themselves that the charity will be efficiently administered. Nor can the Commissioners refuse to register an organization just because it will overlap or even duplicate the work of existing charities or because the name chosen is similar to, or even identical with that of a charity already registered. Some very small charities register pretentious titles including, for example, the word 'National', but the Commissioners can only advise on such matters.

Some attempt to get at a firm definition of 'charity' was made by a working party set up by the National Council of Social Service, at the request of the Charity Commissioners, to consider the possibility of establishing a code of conduct for fund-raising charities (see Chapter 11). The report noted that in everyday usage the words 'charity', 'charitable' and 'charitable purposes' are commonly applied to any enterprise or object associated with welfare as distinct from commercial benefit. The law will, in general, not restrict such claims unless there is evidence of fraudulent intent. It is open to commercial concerns to stretch the meaning of those terms, with impunity, by claiming some charitable object even if they give only a minimum amount of money to it. Even in the case of registered charities there is no universal definition and the legal basis of a charity may sometimes have to be decided by reference to past court decisions, some going back to Elizabethan days.

The 1960 Charities Act does provide a limited definition in section 45 (1): "Any institution, corporate or not, which is established for charitable purposes and is subject to the control of the High Court . . ." When it comes to interpreting what are truly charities the Commissioners and others concerned take into account past common law and revenue decisions which indicate that charity in its legal sense comprises four principal divisions: trusts for the relief of poverty, for the advancement of education, for the advancement of religion, and for other purposes beneficial to the community not falling under the preceding headings.

Between 1868 and 1900 much of the Charity Commissioners' work was making schemes for school charities, but these powers were then given to the Board of Education. Apart from schools, the Board (later the Ministry of Education and finally the Department of Education and Science) administered about 22,000 'recreational' charities, including youth clubs, village halls, recreation grounds, museums and libraries. Control of all these has now gone back to the Commissioners.

The Commissioners *can* be very firm indeed when it comes to accepting a charity for the register and of recent years they have been increasingly worried by bids to establish as 'charities' organizations with political involvement. In one of their annual reports the Commissioners said:

> In a world in which the pace of social change seems ever to be increasing we shall inevitably continue to be faced with new or extended activities the charitable nature of which has never been the subject of consideration by the courts. . . . One contemporary development which has given us some concern has been the increasing desire of voluntary organizations for 'involvement' in the causes with which their work is concerned. Many organizations now feel that it is not sufficient simply to alleviate distress arising from particular social conditions or even to go further and collect and disseminate information about the problems they encounter. They feel compelled also to draw attention as forcibly as possible to the needs which they think are not being met and to press for effective official provision to be made to meet those needs. As a result 'pressure groups', 'action groups' or 'lobbies' come into being. But when a voluntary organization which is a charity seeks to develop such activities it nearly always runs into difficulties through going beyond its declared purposes and powers. No charity should, of course, undertake any activity unless it is reasonably directed to achieving its purposes and is within the powers conferred by the charity's governing instrument.

No trust for the attainment of a political object is a valid charitable trust . . . and any purpose with the object of influencing the legislature is a political purpose.

There have been attempts to get round this rule by describing such wider activities as 'educational' – something that the Commissioners are generally unlikely to accept. There have been instances, particularly in connection with charities concerned with under-developed countries, of over-stepping the boundaries and landing well and truly within the field of propaganda. Say the Commissioners unequivocally: "If a charity with general objects, such as the relief of poverty or distress, issues literature urging the Government to take a particular course or organizes sympathizers to apply pressure for that purpose to their elected representatives, we think it is clear that the boundary has been over-stepped." The Commissioners, however, make it plain that they do not oppose the right of charities to use Parliament to promote or oppose private legislation, such as Private Bills, which vary the conditions of a charity, or to secure powers which only Parliament may confer.

There is also a warning in this report. "If the trustees of a charity do stray into the field of political activity their action will be in breach of trust and those responsible for the action could be called on at law to recoup to the charity any of its funds which have been spent outside its purposes. Moreover, a charity is not entitled to tax relief on income which is not applied to charitable purposes."

Undoubtedly in recent years 'political' activities associated with certain charities have gone some way to damage the 'image' of charity generally. In some cases they have almost destroyed the public view of a given cause. The Commissioners – who have the power to remove from the register any charity proven to have gone beyond its proper functions – touch upon this point. They say:

> It should also be borne in mind that if charities step outside the sphere of activities to which the law confines them, they may not only prejudice the support they receive from some people who could resent the new activities, but they may also eventually endanger the privileged position which charities as a whole have been accorded by the State. The attempts now being made in the United States to curtail the privileges enjoyed by charitable foundations there result in part from allegations that some of those foundations have been using their funds for purposes which are essentially political.

As but one example of their watchdog activities, the Commissioners objected to the payment of £300 to Agitprop, a left-wing organization, by the Student Christian

Movement, on the grounds that it did not appear to have been made for a charitable purpose. They also investigated an interest-free loan to the same organization.

A major instance of cracking down on political activities by charities concerned Sussex University, which was established by Royal Charter in 1961. Article 15 of the charter provided for a students' union with constitution, powers and functions prescribed by university council ordinances. The union was regarded by the Inland Revenue as established for exclusively charitable purposes – its aims included the encouragement and development of the corporate life of the union in cultural, social and athletic fields and the maintenance and extension of friendly relations with other students' unions and with the general public. But in 1971 the Sussex union adopted their own, new constitution in which the objects were defined as being the promotion of any matter whatsoever of interest to its members. And the budget for 1971/72 included proposed payments to War on Want and to a fund for financing a political campaign of protest against the Government's policy of ending certain free milk supplies for school children.

These moves were challenged in court, where Mr Justice Brightman said that the union was clearly an educational charity and it was not therefore open to them to authorize the use of the union's funds for promoting any object which happened to interest the members regardless of whether the object was charitable and educational or not. If union members wished, said the judge, to express their views financially, the money should come from their own personal funds and not from the trust money. Although War on Want was a charity, it was not an educational charity and far less an educational charity connected with students' welfare at Sussex University. It was not open to one charity to subscribe to the funds of another charity unless the recipient charity was expressly or by implication a purpose or object of the donor charity. The proposed milk campaign fund admittedly had a political purpose and was therefore inevitably not charitable, educational or otherwise, because political purposes were not charitable. Charitable funds could not lawfully be used for setting up such a fund.

Another matter which concerns the Commissioners is the attempt by some charities to pursue their affairs in secrecy! Sometimes these are 'private charities', which draw a distinction between organizations where the founder retains in his or his family's hands discretion to select charitable purposes to be helped, and other charities managed by a body of trustees not dominated by the founder. But the Commissioners emphasize that *in law* all charitable trusts are public trusts and have a duty under the Charities Act to provide information to the Commissioners. There may be no obligation to tell other people, but it is much better if they do so in the case of responsible inquirers.

7

'DECAYED' GENTLEFOLK AND OTHER CAUSES

The fascinating charity register maintained by the Commissioners in London's Haymarket spans the centuries. Here are the records of thousands of good intentions, of pious hopes, of noble deeds large and small, some with the highest motives, others born out of pride, dislike, even active hate. It may not be so to the same extent today but in earlier times a charitable trust was one of the best ways of keeping up with Ye Joneses!

Each week between 30 and 40 people visit the registry. Discreetly, the staff decline to analyze their visitors but it is probable that rather more come to *seek* money than to *give* it. Individuals who think they may have some claims on a specialist charity – such as one for indigent former housekeepers, or one for retired professors of Greek – turn up to go through the classified lists of causes. Not only individuals: charities seeking donations from the big trusts send someone along to see whether there is a wealthy organization of some kind or another which is likely to help them. And one great advantage of being on the official records is that these big trusts invariably ask first 'Are you registered?' Of course there are also the people who plan to set up some form of charity and who come along to see if their ground is already covered or to consult the staff on ways and means of achieving their aims.

Apart from the major national charities, there are thousands of small ones, many with intriguing names, strange objectives, and very little money. In olden days when a landlord sold a piece of ground he very often eased his conscience at making a very substantial profit by attaching a 'rent charge' as a condition of the deal. Or perhaps his motives could be pious. The buyer contracted to pay, say, five pounds a year to a nominated charity or set aside a sum which produced five pounds a year. It was something like ground rent for leasehold properties. Remember that in medieval days five pounds was quite a fair sum of money.

The Charity Commissioners are ceaslessly trying to get rid of rent charges because the minute annual income is relatively valueless, can cost as much to collect, and could even lapse if not paid for a certain number of years. Sometimes also people simply and genuinely forget to pay up. Even these tiny charities are supposed to send in annual accounts (if registered) but in practice the Commissioners may often be satisfied with accounts every five years, which at least enables them to check if a given fund has lapsed or been forgotten.

Some of these charities have an annual income as low as 12½p and the Commissioners encourage trustees of small organizations to come to an arrangement with the rent charge donor to settle for a lump sum and abandon the yearly income. There are powers under the Charities Act for compulsory redemption of rent charges but the Commissioners impose a maximum limit for redemption of £20 a year on rent charges producing not less than five pounds a year so that the most the original charity has to find is £300. Working tirelessly through the archives, they have so far organized the release in this fashion of well over 1,000 rent charges.

Even so there are hundreds upon hundreds of small charities still living on money from the long-past and by no means obsolescent – the popular idea that there are vast sums, millions of pounds perhaps, lying hidden away in out-dated charities is simply not true. The majority of them are administered by parsons of various denominations and very typical is the 'Pretty Maid Charity', of Holsworth, Devon, currently administered by the Reverend J. Richards, Rector of the church of St Peter and St Paul. In 1841 – it is by no means one of the really ancient ones – the Reverend Thomas Meyrick left an endowment of £100, which provides to this day a sum of £2.50 each year, 'for the young single woman resident in the parish of Holsworthy, under 30 years of age and generally esteemed by the young as the most deserving, most handsome and most noted for her quietness and attendance at the church.' Annually, in the week following St Peter's feast day, St Peter's Fair is held in the parish and at noon on the Wednesday of the fair the rector emerges from the belfry door to declare the name of the year's Pretty Maid. Comments the rector: "It is a pleasant custom . . . on the other hand I find the choice rather invidious when there are six girls all deserving the honour. The choice is made by a committee, normally consisting of myself and one other. I generally consult the church wardens."

Often these old wills produce problems. A deed made by John White on 26 June 1586 provides for 'Twelve penny loaves to be given to 12 poor persons attending the parish church of Lostwithiel, Cornwall.' They were to receive the loaves after morning service every Sunday. 'The sum of 6/8d to be paid to the Minister of the Parish for preaching a sermon on charity on the last Sunday in August and 1/4d to the clerk for distributing the bread.' You can't get a loaf for a penny, or even a roll, these days, and what happens now is that an annual sum of £3 is paid from the charity to the mayor of Plymouth who in turn passes it on to the mayor of Lostwithiel who hands it over to the vicar, currently the Reverend E.B. Warren, who has to preach the yearly sermon. The money goes in cash to the poor. A similar charity still on the register is that set up in 1705 by Thomas Sewell of Great Henney, Essex, providing for three penny loaves for the three poorest people going to Henney church every Lord's Day.

But it was cakes and ale for the people of Sellack, Ross-on-Wye, Herefordshire. Known now as the 'Pax Cakes', this charity was a rent charge on a local property of five shillings a year, granted by Lady Scudamore in 1658, to be distributed on Palm Sunday at Sellack church and at the daughter church at King's Caple. Says the vicar, the Reverend E. Hugh Moseley: "The distribution of cakes has been performed since the charity's institution, except that between 1914 and 1918 buns were used. I don't know when the ale was discontinued!"

There are scores of charities for the maintenance of tombstones and suchlike and as many for the provision of flannel, which appears to have been a favourite Victorian gift. There is, for example, the 1869 fund for flannel for the poor of Liskeard, Cornwall, and the 1896 fund for 'the purchase of Welsh flannel for distribution annually in October among the aged poor residing in the parish of Denby, Derbyshire.' Wolverton, Buckinghamshire, has an 1881 charity for the provision of cloaks and bonnets for widows and single women of not less than 60 years of age, while in 1812 William Selwood left money for 'foul weather jackets' for the poor men of Cumnor, Berkshire. Red flannel at Christmas is stipulated in an 1817 charity at Pleaseley, Derbyshire. Other charities provide outfits for apprentices and the 1680 will of Robert Barnard of Belton, in the Isle of Axholme, Lincolnshire, left a small amount to 'give to the poor of the Parish of Belton yearly for ever 120 yards of blue prast carsey and to provide wheaten bread to the poor.'

In 1738 John Courtenay Bonus left a sum producing between five pounds and ten pounds annually to provide one pint of beer, stout or cider each Christmas to poor persons of good character, of 60 years or over who had lived in the parish of Alphington, Devonshire, for at least five years. Richard and Edmund Stevenson, of Dronfield, Derbyshire, set up a fund in 1577 to supply bread and fish on each Friday in Lent while in 1864 Richard Belcher wrote a cautionary proviso into his will. He left a few pounds to pay the minister of the parish of Wantage, Berkshire, 15s to preach a sermon on St Matthias' Day and another pound or two to provide bread for the poor of the Established Church. But if the minister did not preach, then the poor got his 15s also!

The Catharine Fisher Charity provides for the payment of five shillings each to 40 poor housekeepers living in Manchester who constantly attend Divine Service of the Church of England, 24 penny loaves for distribution every Sunday in the Collegiate Church of Manchester, and 30 penny loaves every Good Friday, Ascension Day and Christmas Day. She also provided for distribution of £2.10s among ten poor housekeepers living in Salford and attending church.

Cautious was Ann Beaumont of Hadleigh, Suffolk, in 1701, when she left two pounds a year for caps and neck cloths for four poor aged men and four poor aged women, she left another two pounds 'to defray the charges of a dinner of the trustees at the yearly audit'!

One could go on and on, but let us cite just one more example of this kind of charity. In 1809 John Wagstaffe, of Bawburgh, Norfolk, provided in his will for the annual purchase of a silver spoon, value 18s., to be given to any couple of 'labouring poor' married at Bawburgh on the birth of their first child.

Something other than plain good intentions can be seen in a study of some of these old bequests, and a few modern ones. There was – is? – quite extraordinary snobbishness and prejudice among some 'charitable' persons, with their fondness for such phrases as 'decayed gentlewoman' and their liking for maidenhood and the 'middle and upper classes'. Typical of this attitude is the 1813 will which benefited 'persons in the middle ranks of life who have become reduced in circumstances' while as late as 1930 Mary Elizabeth Adams provided pensions of not less than £20 and not more than £34 a year for 'decayed and worth Gentlewomen whether widows or spinsters of not less than 50 years who have resided in Plymouth for ten years or more and are not of the Jewish religion or profess the tenets of the Roman Catholic faith.'

In 1946 Eva Clare Davidson left money for 'flats for the use of gentlewomen (in the Victorian sense of the word and not retired nurses or schoolteachers unless the above term should apply strictly) in reduced circumstances.' If that be thought ambiguous, consider the will of one William Fisher who bequeathed annuities 'for ladies in reduced circumstances who shall be persons believing in the Unity of God or members of the Roman Catholic Church.' The Gentlewomen's Holiday Guild, Tunbridge Wells, Kent, exists to provide fortnight's holidays for 'gentlewomen of birth and education' while Caroline Harper left an annuity in 1937 to 'needy gentlewomen of good character having limited incomes and not being either Roman Catholics, Jewesses, Spiritualists or members of "a Socialist Party".'

Some of these charities for gentlefolk, decayed or otherwise, have minute incomes but quite a few receive thousands a year still in donations, and one has so much money it cannot spend that each Spring it sends two of its officials on a sort of Grand Tour of Europe, seeking out elderly English ladies on the Riviera and similar places to whom they can hand out cash!

'Charity' may mean 'love' but, under British law it is also charitable to kill. One of the headings in the classified lists in the Haymarket is 'Promotion of the efficiency of the Forces' and there is a curious tale behind it. During the South African War British soldiers on the whole had a shockingly bad reputation as marksmen – many of them just could not hit the elusive Boer. Some loyal Britons established a fund to help train the country's soldiers to shoot straight and thus kill more of the enemy. When they applied for charity registration such patriotic aims were held to be a valid charitable purpose, as education, and this set an invaluable precedent for the innumerable rifle clubs and Service amenity organizations of today. For example, the Royal Tournament with its annual income of around £16,000 is a charity because its aims include raising funds 'to benefit various Naval, Marine, Army and Air Force charities, to popularize the Services and, to a limited extent, to promote skill-at-arms in all ranks of Her Majesty's Naval, Marine, Army and Air Forces.' There is, on the same precedent, a charity for the repair of trophies and relics presented to the Royal Navy and for the replacement of lost or destroyed trophies. A typical rifle club charity will have as its declared aims 'To encourage skill in rifle shooting by any of Her Majesty's subjects so that they will be better fitted to serve their country.'

Rifle clubs and similar organizations apart, the Services give the Charity Commissioners a good deal of work. The rundown of the Armed Forces over recent years and the constant redeployment of units has meant that many regimental and similar charities have had to be re-allocated to central funds or re-formed corps, or two or three particular regimental charities merged into one.

Analysis of the charity register indicates that well over half of all charities have a yearly income of less than £100; about 23 per cent have less than five pounds; and about six percent more than £5,000 a year. Of *new* charities, about 25 per cent expect an income of less than £100 a year and about nine per cent expect more than £5,000. Only three per cent of new charities are established for 'moral welfare and reform'.

8

AS NEAR AS POSSIBLE . . .

Though, as has been said, it is not true that millions of pounds lie tucked away in old charities that have lost their original purpose, been overtaken by events, or have just been forgotten, there certainly must be in the aggregate many thousands of pounds that could be re-deployed. There is one town in the West Country which has an ancient charity designed to provide 'almshouses' for the local poor. Today there are definitely no 'poor' in this town and, say the trustees, "Even if there were we dare not build homes and call them 'almshouses'." The fund continues to accumulate by something like £100 a year. There is another charitable fund in the same town which was set up to provide books for local scholars. With books provided free in most schools, there is every year more money coming in to the fund than applications for assistance. Told about the work of the Charity Commissioner's cy-près schemes, the very elderly chairman of the trustees admitted that he never knew the original aims of a charity could be changed to take account of modern circumstances, and he added, "Well, the money's safe and, you never know, we might need it some day . . ."

There have been cases – now largely cleared up – of money left to supply coal for poor persons or distressed gentlefolk who now live in smokeless zones, in all-electric or centrally heated council flats and so on. No real excuse exists for preserving such out-dated charities; the Commissioners, the 'doctors of charity', exist to cure just these sort of ills.

Before the Charitable Trusts Act of 1860 the Chancery Court had the power to alter the purposes of endowed charities when they could no longer be carried out. This was done by means of the cy-près scheme – the Norman-French term for 'as near as possible to'. But the rules were somewhat constrictive: such schemes might be made only in circumstances amounting to total failure of the charity concerned. The restrictions continued until the Charities Act of 1960, which permits cy-près schemes under a variety of different circumstances. Schemes may be made to allow the property of two or more charities with similar purposes to be made applicable for common purposes; to redefine in modern terms the area in which a charity operates or the class of persons it may benefit; and even to prescribe new purposes when it can be shown that the original aims are totally impracticable or adequately provided for by other means.

Schemes may also be made where the original purposes cease to provide an effective method of using the property available from the gift 'having regard to the spirit of the gift'. This phrase is important and was considered by the High Court in the case of Repton's Charity in 1971. The court laid down a valuable interpretation of Section 13 of the Charities Act. The case concerned the bequest in 1715 of a plot of land to be held on trust to pay out of the rents three pounds a year to the minister of the Independent Chapel at Pudsey, Yorkshire, with the balance left over each year to go to the poor and aged of the town. In 1715 the land produced a total income of five pounds a year.

Under a cy-près scheme the land was sold a few years ago and the proceeds invested, yielding £791 a year. At the start of the new scheme, however, the local minister still received only the three pounds a year laid down in the original will. Understandably, he was not very satisfied and the matter went to court. The judge referred to Section 13 of the Act and its doctrine that regard should be had to the 'spirit of the gift' and he held that these words referred to the underlying intention of a donor. In this case it appeared that the intention was to divide the available money so that the minister would receive three-fifths of it, a modest but not negligible sum at the time. This condition, said the judge, was plainly defeated when, in current conditions, the minister took a derisory £3 out of a total of £791. But the judge also had to consider whether the gift fell into two parts – one specifically stipulating payment of three pounds to the minister and the other dealing with the residue. He concluded that where a testator disposed of the entire income of a fund for charitable purposes it was natural to speak of the disposition as a single charitable gift even though the gift was for more than one charitable purpose. Having found that the gift of land to provide an income for both the minister and the poor was one gift, he decided that the minister should receive £100 a year, which was accepted by all parties.

Since 1960 the Commissioners have been able to meet most of the well-founded applications that have received to alter or enlarge the purpose of a charity but they have also turned down applications such as a proposed change of purpose to a quite different field of charitable activity. When, for example, a charity was set up to provide penny loaves, money for poor emigrants, or some such out-dated cause, the Commissioners substitute provisions permitting the charity to use its money for ways which still relieve need in whatever form it may be found to exist, since the basic intention of donors was usually to make a real contribution to relieving distress. Many charities were established for the repair of roads and bridges, matters now handled by local authorities, and the Commissioners here substitute other general purposes for the benefit of local inhabitants which could include promotion of the arts, provision of seats or shelters, the preservation of old buildings or the improvement of local amenities.

One reason why many obsolescent charities fail to take advantage of these schemes appears to be that they are *afraid* to approach the Commissioners in case they are penalized for not carrying out their trusts strictly. But the Commissioners take the view that there is nothing to penalize where trustees depart from their rules in the honest belief that what they are doing is better for the community they serve: failure to keep within a trust may often be evidence of the need to alter its purpose rather than of dereliction of duty on the part of the trustees.

There are still, however, trustees who are lazy or blindly satisfied with what they are doing. They do not appear to know that Section 13 of the 1960 Act lays a duty on trustees to make the charity effective and that under Section 18 the Commissioners can, if they wish, make a scheme on their own accord, although they have not found it necessary to do so yet.

There have been cases of local accident funds where the money subscribed proved over-generous and for years the balance lay dormant because it could not be disposed of. Sometimes money is raised for a cause which in the event, proves impracticable. Section 14 of the Act provides that if donors to a fund that cannot carry out its purpose any longer cannot be located, or if they can be found and they execute a disclaimer of their right to have their donations or properties returned, the donor can be deemed to have had a *general* charitable intention so that the money they gave can be dealt with by a cy-près scheme.

The effect of the Act in liberalizing cy-près schemes is seen in the fact that the average number of schemes made by the Commissioners annually in the ten years before the Act was 516 and in the ten years after it 701. In 1972 about 870 schemes were set up.

Social change – and the increasing wealth of some charities – are mirrored in the following four examples. The Religious Society of Friends approached the Commissioners to report that they held £15,430, comprising a gift of £10,000 made by a Mr Robert McDougall in 1933, and accumulated income. The original gift was made to the Friends' Allotment Committee fund set up in 1930 to help unemployed men by providing allotment land, seeds and implements. But today the demand for allotments is minimal and a new scheme permits the Friends to use surplus money from the fund to help the unemployed in such ways as the society thinks fit.

John Townsend and John Ward, of the parish of Old, Northamptonshire, established charities in 1668 and 1707. Land given by the men for the benefit of the poor of the parish was sold in 1971 to the Northampton Development Corporation for £238,000, enormously increasing the twin charities' income. The Commissioners produced a scheme in 1972 widening the aims so that up to one-third of the income may be applied to promote the education of needy parishioners of Old, without age limit, for example by provision of scholarships, outfits, books or tools, recreational facilities and so on. The balance of the fund may be applied to general relief for the needy of the parish where provision is not made out of the rates, taxes or other public funds.

The Ursula Lodges Trust was established in Sidcup, Kent, in 1854 to provide dwellings for spinster members of the Church of England, 45 years of age or older and with an income of not less than £50 and not more than £100 a year. Over the years the buildings fell into a bad state of repair and the trustees simply did not have the resources to undertake the necessary work. The Charity Commissioners appointed as new trustees in 1971 the Chislehurst and Mottingham Housing Association, which was looking for a site for development. A lease of the charity land was then granted for 99 years at an annual rent of five pounds, to a new charitable housing association, the Sidcup Housing Association, specially set up for the purpose. The new scheme still covers poor spinsters of not less than 45 years of age, but without the limitation on income, and it also provides that if there are not enough suitable Church of England applicants, vacancies may be filled by others. The original six cottages were to be demolished and 40 centrally heated flats built, with a communal room, television room, geriatric bathroom, chiropody room, and a warden's flat.

A charity which grew too rich for its original purpose began in 1868 with a bequest of £10,000 by one Catharine Wright. The charity became the 'Liverpool Merchants' Guild' in 1914, with the object of granting pensions to aged and distressed members of the 'upper and middle classes of society' who had lived in Liverpool for not less than 15 years. Many gifts were made to the Guild and by the 1970s the aggregate value of property administered was about £1.8m, producing an annual income of about £70,000. It was impossible to use all this for pensions and under the new scheme produced by the Commissioners the charity receives wide discretion not only in paying pensions but in making money grants or providing in other ways for members of the 'upper and middle' classes residing in or near the City of Liverpool for not less than 15 years and who are at least 50 years of age.

Then there is the re-formation of a 'Penitent Prostitutes' charity! The Magdalen Hospital Act 1768 set up a corporation to govern a hospital at St George's Fields, Southwark, in South London, for 'the reception of Penitent Prostitutes', their maintenance and employment. About a hundred years later this was replaced by a new hospital in Streatham, South London, and by 1934 that had become a senior approved school for girls under the Children and Young Persons Act of 1933. This, in its turn, was closed in 1966. The Charity Commissioners permitted the land and premises to be sold to the Greater London Council for £250,000 and then had to find ways of using the money. A new scheme was brought into operation in 1973 by which the charity income is devoted to promoting the welfare of young persons exposed to moral danger or prevented by any circumstances from providing properly for themselves or their children. Any surplus income may be used for preventing crime and delinquency among young people in need of care, control or protection by reason of environmental or other circumstances, including research into the causes of delinquency. It is interesting to note how closely the scheme relates to the original intentions of the founders of more than 200 years ago and yet deals with the situation in current terms.

Certain charities are regulated or controlled by acts of Parliament and once, if a change were desired, the charity had to secure a Private Act. Today the Commissioners operate a system confirmed by statutory instruments made by the Home Secretary. If the scheme alters a statutory provision of a Public General Act it must be approved by resolution of each House of Parliament; in other cases there is 'negative' control — a scheme may be annulled by resolution of either House within 40 days of being laid. The Town Moor Money Charity is an interesting example.

From time immemorial resident freemen of Newcastle-upon-Tyne and their widows had been entitled to grazing rights over land known as the Town Moor, but in 1774 as the result of a dispute with the Corporation, a Private Act of Parliament was passed, enclosing part of the Moor, letting-off, and distributing the rents among poor resident freemen and poor resident widows of freemen of the city. By 1967 many problems had arisen and the Charity Commissioners were consulted. With soaring land values, the charity's income had risen tremendously but there were actually also increasing limits on what could be done with it. Because of slum clearance and other reasons a number of the original recipients now lived outside the city boundary. Furthermore, the amount which could be given to each beneficiary without relieving public funds — something that is distinctly *not* the objective of charities — was limited to the amount which may be disregarded in calculating social security benefits. The trustees also wished to provide relief other than by monetary payments.

In May 1970 a new scheme, under Section 19 of the Act, was brought into operation. The income may now go to poor freemen and poor widows and daughters of freemen of the city in conditions of need, hardship or distress, not only by money grants but by providing or paying for items, services or facilities calculated to reduce their need. The original requirement that beneficiaries should live in the city was not included in the new scheme but a direction was given that the trustees give preference to beneficiaries living either in the city or in the counties of Durham and Northumberland. Under the scheme also the number of trustees was reduced from about 60 to seven.

Quite apart from their own direct work, the Charity Commissioners assist in a widespread local review of charities in which most of the administrative counties of England and Wales have taken part. These local reviews arise from Sections 10, 11 and 12 of the Charities Act which were the outcome of considerable discussion on the part which charities should play after post-war social legislation had resulted in the traditional benefits provided by private charity being largely replaced by the Welfare State. Broadly, it was decided that while charity should not withdraw from any field where it was performing a useful service, its special function was to seek out the gaps in the social services and to pioneer new services. The sections of the Act were based on the principle that the resources of voluntary organizations should remain at their own disposal and co-operation between them and the statutory services should be on the basis of partnership, not subordination. The Act therefore authorizes local authorities to maintain a charity index, to review non-ecclesiastical charities, and to make arrangements for co-ordinating the work of the local authority with charities providing similar services.

The Commissioners issued guidance to local authorities conducting these reviews, which are a continuing process, and defined the aims of such reviews to ensure (1) that there is no duplication between the work of two charities in one area; (2) that charities complement and do not duplicate the work and benefits of the statutory welfare services; and (3) that charity income is used to give the most effective help to those in need whom – for whatever reason – the statutory services cannot help in the way required.

The reviews showed up many cases calling for the Commissioners' cy-près schemes and discovered some charities which should have registered but failed to do so. A striking instance of what can emerge from the reviews is the Winchester and Rural District Welfare Trust, which now combines no less than 26 charities in 13 different parishes, with the area of benefit extended to 25 parishes in the district. The capital of the constituent charities – mostly invested in 2½ per cent Consolidated Stock – was re-invested, mainly in the Official Investment Fund, and the old system of handing out small pensions and gifts at Christmas, so often the stock-in-trade of parochial charities, was replaced by a policy of worthwhile grants in cases of real need. Before the merger, ten of the charities had an annual income of less than five pounds each. Today the Trust's annual income is around £350. And the sort of thing they do with the money admirably illustrates the idea of plugging the gaps in the Social Services. £100 provided radio earphones in an old people's ward, a grant was made for the hire of a TV set for an elderly house-bound woman, electric warning bells were provided for elderly and infirm people living in the area, a ramp was bought to enable a cancer sufferer to get into her garden.

By the end of 1972 a total of 560 'unification' schemes had been made by the Commissioners as the result of local reviews in eight years.

There are many other fascinating re-organization schemes in the Commissioners' records. The Corporation of the Sons of the Clergy, founded in 1678 to help poor widows and children of the 'Clergie in England', finding that there was insufficient demand for assistance from their charter funds, wished to widen their scope and under the Commissioners' scheme the Corporation may now help also clergymen of the Church of England and of any church in full communion with the C. of E., and their dependants. The Richmond Parish Charity Lands (1785) and The Highland Society of London (1778) are two more examples of modernization and there are numerous mergers of small church parochial charities in the City of London. A classic case of what might be called a 'lost cause' is Lord Craven's Charity, founded by the will of John, Lord Craven, dated 28 May 1647. At that time there was still an element of 'holy war' between Christianity and Islam and Lord Craven provided that out of the rents of property in Sussex four scholarships of £25 per annum each should be paid towards the maintenance of two poor scholars at the University of Cambridge and two at the University of Oxford. He then directed that the residue of the income from the property be paid 'towards the redemption of English Christian captive prisoners in Algiers or other places under the dominion of the Turks'. The Barbary pirates did in fact raid right up the English Channel until finally defeated by the Royal Navy in 1816. The charity could not continue and no money was spent on captives after 1886. Over the years various changes were made: the land in Sussex was sold, the money invested, and the amount devoted to the educational side of the trust was greatly increased. But there were no powers to alter the provision for Christian captives. It was, by 1950, also considered that the case for transferring unused funds to educational purposes was becoming weaker with the continuing growth of State education. The Charity Commissioners found the answer in 1968, when they produced a scheme whereby the 'captives' money would go for the relief of Christian Britons who are or have been prisoners-of-war in any of the countries bordering on the Mediterranean and are in distress or who, never being prisoners-of-war, have otherwise suffered severe distress in any of those countries.

The Commissioners can indeed be very ingenious – and sometimes they display an unexpected sense of humour! Take the Charity of Sir Samuel Lennard, St John the Baptist, West Wickham, Kent. In 1618 Sir Samuel's will declared that

> As by Act of Parliament the 5th November is ordered to be a day of thanksgiving for God's deliverance of this country from the Powder Treason, for the better continuance of the memory of God's merciful deliverance from that infernal and damnable treason plotted or contrived by the Satanic lymbes of that anti-Christian and hereticke of Rome, a sermon is to be preached on the said 5th November of every year in the Parish Church of West Wickham; the 129th and 127th psalms to be sung; and the preacher to rehearse in the pulpit the names and condition of those wretches that were actors in that treason . . . Twenty Shillings yearly to be paid to the preacher immediately after the sermon and 12d each to 40 persons present. In case of default of payment the land to be distrained for the amount. Of the poor recipients of this bounty, 15 are to be from West Wickham, 10 of Keston, 10 of Hayes and 5 from Farnborough to be nominated (by Sir Samuel's heirs) from the honestest sort of the poor of those parishes.

The original endowment was a yearly rent charge of three pounds which was later redeemed for £120 in 2½ per cent Consolidated Stock, now held by the Official Custodian for Charities. The Commissioners decided that the three pounds should be applied to the upkeep of the parish church of St John the Baptist at West Wickham. "We had to decide," they said, "whether the purpose of the gift of two pounds to be distributed to 40 poor persons attending the service was the advancement of religion or the relief of poverty and we concluded that the real spirit of the gift was to encourage the potential recipients to attend church and that it was therefore a gift for the advancement of religion."

9

UNITIES AND RIVALRIES

Apart from legal and historical complexities, there are often human problems in re-organizing and merging charities. Charity organizers, trustees and officials mostly have a considerable degree of self-esteem, not always warranted. There is a widespread fear of loss of identity in mergers . . . "People know our name, they've always given to *us*, we'll lose all our donations and legacies if we merge", many say. The other great objection is that aims are laid down strictly and must not be confused with any other charitable intentions, but this can generally be got around by a cy-près scheme, provided the charities have more or less the same intent. The Commissioners also have a way round the individual identity problem.

They can set up a single body of trustees to administer a number of charities, leaving them in all other respects as separate bodies, each with its own objects. But they prefer when possible to secure closer union by a scheme establishing a common purpose or set of purposes. Sometimes, then, they prepare a scheme which results in the various organizations becoming a single charity with undivided endowments, laying it down that 'the charities shall be administered and managed together as one charity under the name . . . .' There was at one time some doubt about this procedure because it was felt that the method could lead to a situation where people thought an individual charity had died and that people paying out legacies and donations would need to be satisfied that they could safely pay to the trustees of a united charity a legacy left by name to one of the individual bodies.

However, as far back as 1912 the Court of Appeal laid it down that while the form and purpose of an endowed charity might be changed by due process of law, the charity itself could not be destroyed or extinguished. The Commissioners decided that their formula 'administered and managed together as one charity' did not extinguish the charities involved and that while it permitted consolidation of the endowments and maintenance of a single set of accounts, the constituent charities continued to exist.

When one considers uniting charities with similar aims there is also the question of overlapping appeals, something that noticeably irritates large sections of the public and a matter which also reflects the self-esteem of charitable organizations. Something has been done. The Royal National Institute for the Blind (see Chapter 17) has a co-ordinatd scheme which works excellently; the Central Council for the Disabled is now an umbrella organization of some 300 bodies working in one way or another for the disabled. But rivalries and charity power politics play a major part in this problem. The National Council of Social Service working party report on charitable fund-raising recorded complaints both to the Charity Commissioners and the Home Office about appeals by national charities conflicting with local needs in what seemed to be much the same field. The working party referred to 'numerous complaints', particularly from local councils of social service.

These local appeals may consist of house-to-house collections or street collections. About 100 charities possess an exemption certificate from the Home Office, which frees them from having to get the consent of the local authority and they are the main sources of wrath since the national organizers do not have to consult locally but just sail into an area *en masse* with their collecting boxes!

Said the working party report: "We suggest that the Home Office be recommended to survey afresh all the procedures involved in the granting of exemption certificates to national charities. It appears that this is a routine which has been going on for a long time and is not always clear to the charities or the public. The number of charities having exemption certificates should perhaps be limited. Provision should also be made to look carefully at the extent to which charities are using these certificates, perhaps reviewing them periodically. The criteria adopted when considering the granting or withdrawal of exemption certificates should also be examined and made known." The report observed that these certificates did make it possible to make economic national appeals and the charities concerned would be loathe to relinquish the practice.

Often the public ask "Why can't one central fund collect on behalf of all charities of a given kind, like cancer and so forth?" There is no straight answer. As has already been discussed, people are very possessive about their own pet causes and dislike the impersonality, as they see it, of central funds. Two conflicting views were reported by the working party. The Royal National Institute for the Blind gave evidence: "We feel very strongly from our own experience that amalgamation for fund-raising purposes of a number of charities operating in a similar field must reduce costs and irritation to the public and, by strengthening the appeal, lead to greater sums being raised for the benefit of the participating charities."

In contrast, the Royal Alfred Merchant Seamen's Society said:

> As it happens, in the case of marine charities we have one central fund (King George's Fund for Sailors) and they are responsible for raising the bulk of our needs. Despite this splendid central organization, they are not able to provide all the money required and in any event people still like to choose their individual charity and not donate centrally for general distribution . . . It is also a basic fact that the difference between a deficit and a surplus on the accounts for the year is usually covered by legacies and therefore, to survive, each individual charity must do its own advertising.

Overlapping is far from the only complaint voiced by the public and by the charities themselves. There is the constant proliferation of new charities, all seeking their slice of the cake, even though money does not seem inexhaustible. The Charity Commissioners do not by any means approve all applications for registration, though, as explained earlier, their powers in this respect are limited. In the ten years between 1960 and 1970 they rejected applications from no less than 1,352 organizations and removed from the register 381, all but four of which had ceased to operate. In the four cases they decided that the objects were not charitable.

All sorts of concerns, mostly highly respectable, seek to secure the benefits of charity registration – rates and tax reliefs and the right to approach the foundations for instance. There have been some notable failures to get on the list.

Take the Bath Club Servants' Benevolent Fund. The Commissioners reported:

> Although 'benevolent' when defining purposes of an organization is regarded as too wide to be charitable, the phrase 'benevolent fund' is so frequently used as part of the title of funds for poor members of a particular class that the use of these words in the title of a fund raises the expectation that the fund will be charitable. This was not,

however, found to be so in the case of the Bath Club Servants' Benevolent Fund because, as inspection of the rules showed, its grants were not confined to the relief of poverty since the committee administering the fund could equally well use it for rewarding meritorious service.

Then there was the case of the Charitable Catering Society Limited. Said the Commissioners:

> The promoters of the Charitable Catering Society Limited were aware that many charities, such as voluntary hospitals, nursing homes and old people's homes, which provide meals for their beneficiaries encounter some difficulty in obtaining the services of suitable catering staff. It was in the hope of giving assistance to such charities that this company was formed with a declared purpose of advancing the work of such charitable institutions by the provision at cost of catering staff for them. The company would therefore operate solely for the benefit of charities and it accordingly sought registration as a charity. It seemed to us, however, that the provision of a service for charities is not necessarily a charitable purpose of itself, nor in the present case could this purpose be regarded as merely ancillary to any particular charitable purpose. We therefore decided not to register the company as a charity because we did not consider that the provision of catering staff at cost was a charitable purpose even when the service was limited to charities.

Unlucky also was the National House-Builders Registration Council, which has as its principal object the improvement of the house-building industry throughout the United Kingdom. The Commissioners found:

> On perusal of the memorandum of association it turned out that one of the main purposes of the association was the compilation of a register of house-builders who in the opinion of the association observed and maintained a sufficiently high standard of house-building. It was claimed that this was to be compiled in order to protect ordinary people who employed builders and we were told that the association has been set up with Government encouragement; but from other clauses in the memorandum it was clear that house-builders were themselves likely to derive direct benefit from the association. We came to the conclusion that on balance the association conferred more benefit on those engaged in the industry than it did on the public and that it could not therefore be regarded as an altruistic organization.

In another application a firm of solicitors asked for registration of two trusts whose objects were 'for the benefit of any charitable object or purpose that the trustees may deem proper'. Apart from the fact that the Commissioners do not favour wide general terms to express the purpose of a charity, here the trustees would have been empowered to grant leases – which could have gone to a trustee – without any restriction on term, purpose, rent or conditions. The trustees could also invest funds on personal credit, acquire property not producing an income and carry on any trade, business or undertaking connected or proposed to be connected with the trust fund. The deeds did lay it down that nothing contained in them should authorize the application of any part of the income or capital of the trust fund for any object or purpose that was not charitable. The Commissioners rejected the application, concluding that "the powers were so wide that, while acting strictly within them, it would be lawful for the trustees so to deal with the property that any one of them or his nominee could derive substantial personal benefit."

Successful though were the Cistercian monks of Caldey Abbey on Caldey Island, off Tenby, Pembrokeshire. The case here depended on a nice point. Clearly the abbey is devoted to the promotion of the Roman Catholic religion but the question was whether the benefit was conferred solely on the enclosed community of monks or on the public. In the case of at least one enclosed Order the Commissioners had ruled previously that a public charity did not exist. The monks of Caldey produced evidence that the services in their abbey church are open to the public at all times and that priests are sent out to help parishes on the mainland. The Commissioners decided that all this was a public benefit and agreed to registration.

Also successful were the Botanical Society of the British Isles and the Northumberland and Durham Naturalists' Trust who raised funds to appeal to a public inquiry against the proposed construction of a large reservoir in Upper Teesdale. In the event no public inquiry was held and the fund ended up with a surplus which it intended to use for conservation work in Upper Teesdale. Was this a charity? It was argued that the purpose of the fund was political insofar as it was to oppose a change in the law and to oppose the Private Bill promoted by the Tees Valley and Cleveland Water Board. On considering the case, the Commissioners reported: "We came to the conclusion that the evidence showed that the purpose of the fund was the preservation of the flora and fauna of Upper Teesdale which was an undoubtedly charitable purpose. We also concluded that there was no objection to the trustees using the fund in furtherance of its purposes in opposing a Private Bill . . . it does not seem to us that such action comes within the objection to charities pursuing political purposes."

10

TAKEN TO COURT

During recent years there have been a number of High Court decisions on charity matters. One of the most important was a dual case centred around what happens when charities are thought by contestants to get too much out of a will. The Charity Commissioners are often asked by charity trustees to permit voluntary payments to meet what appears to the trustees to be valid moral obligations even though they have no legal basis. Trustees have, for instance, wished to make an *ex gratia* payment where the intentions of some testator have been frustrated by some facet of the law of wills, with the result that the charity received a large legacy at the expense of a person who had lost his claim to a legacy obviously intended for him. For long it was held by the Commissioners and by the Attorney-General that *ex-gratia* payments such as this could not be made by trustees. But this had not been firmly laid down by the courts and so the Attorney-General encouraged the plaintiffs in two applications to go to court so that the matter could be treated as a test case.

In what may be called the 'Snowden case' the testator gave to relatives all his shares in certain companies and left the residue of the estate to a number of charities. But the companies were taken over, the testator's shares sold, and at the time of his death were represented in his estate by *cash.* This meant that there were no *shares* to go to the relatives – they got nothing at all – but the legacies to the charities were considerably enhanced. Most, but not all, of the charities involved felt that they had a moral obligation to make some payment to the relatives, arguing that since charities rely for their subscriptions on recognition by the public of a moral duty to support charities, so also charities cannot and must not ignore moral obligations that are laid on them, and should behave in this respect at least as well as a responsible individual.

The 'Henderson case' was different. Here the testatrix made a will to which some words had been added in her handwriting but in a different colour ink. It was uncertain whether these words had been added before execution of the will and they were not recognized, although they would have had a considerable effect in increasing the size of legacies payable to a nephew and a niece. The will ended with the words 'Anything over to Charitys' (*sic*). The executrix asked the court to permit her to pay increased legacies to the nephew and niece to meet the wishes expressed in the additional words, even though this would cut out the residue left, in the main body of the will, to charities.

Mr Justice Cross came to the important conclusion that the court and the Attorney-General *had* the power to give authority to charity trustees to make *ex-gratia* payments out of funds held on charitable trusts. He did not suggest that the trustees could do this themselves without authority. He did emphasize that such authority is not to be granted on slender grounds, but only in cases where it could be fairly said that if the charity were an individual it would be morally wrong for him to refuse to make the payment. He drew the distinction between cases like those before him, in which the testator never intended the charity to receive so much, and a case in which the testator did intend the charity to get exactly what came to it but the relatives considered they should have the money. In the latter case there would be, as a rule, no moral obligation resting on the charity and no authority should be given for it to make a payment.

After this decision there were five cases in which charities applied to the Commissioners to make *ex-gratia* payments, and the Attorney-General agreed to all of them.

Charity critics often cite 'Poor Relations rackets', by which it is popularly believed that a man may leave money to his relatives under a charitable trust, to their considerable advantage. In fact this sort of thing is watched extremely closely! The difficulty is that a relatively small number of beneficiaries may constitute a sufficiently important section of the public where the object is the relief of poverty, and so be quite valid. In that case this 'Poor Relations' class forms a legal exception to the general rule that to be charitable a trust must be of a public character for the benefit of the community, or a sufficiently important section of it, and not for the benefit of a particular class of private individuals. It was considered that the 'Poor Relations' class extended to any trust fund for the relief of poverty among employees or former employees of an individual or company, even though they might not be a sufficient section of the public to establish charitable status under any other head of charity. This was held established as far back as 1900 in the Gosling case, concerned with pensions for clerks in a banking firm, and the exception was confirmed by the Court of Appeal in 1950 in the case of Gibson *v.* South American Stores Limited, which concerned a trust for a company's necessitous employees and ex-employees and for the dependants of such living or dead beneficiaries.

In 1951 the House of Lords decreed that, apart from 'Poor Relations' cases, a trust should not be regarded as charitable if the benefits under it were confined to the descendants of a named individual or to the employees of a particular individual or company. It was also said that the 'Poor Relations' cases and the Gibson case might need further consideration in the House of Lords on some future occasion. This further consideration came in 1972 in Dingle *v.* Turner and Others, dealing with pensions for poor employees of a limited company. The House of Lords confirmed that both the 'Poor Relations' and 'Poor Employees' trusts constitute valid charitable trusts.

Apart from cases which have to be fought out of court, the Charity Commissioners have considerable powers of their own. They do have teeth, despite some Press assertions to the contrary! It is, for example, Contempt of Court to refuse to supply accounts to the Commissioners. One of the ways in which they are required under the 1960 Act to promote the effective use of charitable resources is by the investigation and checking of abuses. They may themselves institute inquiries or appoint somebody else to make them. They can insist that a charity's accounts are audited by a qualified accountant, and they can suspend or remove a trustee or a servant of a charity. These powers have been used sparingly because there has not been the need. Complaints from the public, or from ex-members of a charity, can usually be dealt with by the co-operation of the trustees concerned.

Some trustees are found to be inexperienced – indeed naïve – but at the opposite end of the scale there have been charities whose trustees have insisted on maintaining a large annual surplus, arguing that their administration was efficient if this surplus was continually rising, and neglecting or deliberately deferring distribution of benefits. There still are a number of such organizations. One, for 'gentlewomen', puts a full half of its annual receipts to capital account and only distributes the other half. There are charities with hundreds of thousands of pounds 'in reserve', a few have millions. But to be fair, when challenged about reserves, most of such charities can point out that with inflation and the falling value of money, they simply must have adequate reserves to cover the future uncertain years. There is a lot in this . . . but not in the case of every charity.

It is obvious that the most popular misconception about charities overall is that they spend far too much on administration and fund-raising, leaving too little for the poor, or sick, or whatever. This point is dealt with at some depth at various points in this book but to some extent any bad image is attributable to many charities' fondness for secrecy and the unnecessarily complicated – sometimes positively deceitful – way in which they present their annual accounts. Very many charities, for instance, show only the *net* revenue from a particular fund-raising activity, and *none* show how much – if any – is paid out in collectors or organizers' commission.

In one of its annual reports the Charity Commissioners dealt to a certain extent with this public anxiety. They said:

> A particular difficulty arises where we receive complaints that the administrative costs of a charity appear to absorb an unduly high proportion of the charity's income so that little is available to apply to the actual objects of the charity . . . It is not possible to lay down any firm rule about the percentage of a charity's income which it can be considered reasonable for it to spend on administration. The administrative expenses of charities necessarily vary greatly. Those of a charity which merely receives money and hands it out again to other organizations should be very low, while those of an organization which itself provides a service of some kind, such as residential homes or advice centres, will necessarily be much higher. Another complication is that a newly-founded charity, which has first to establish an office and then to raise money and build up an organization to achieve its objects, is likely for a period to spend a relatively large part of its income for this purpose. The level of administrative costs in any particular charity must accordingly be looked at in the light of all the circumstances of the particular case. But where these costs seem unreasonably high we take the matter up with the charity and we continue to keep an eye on the developments as long as they may seem necessary.

By far the most notorious of the situations turned up by the Charity Commissioners in their various inquiries was the Sanctuary case. The Commissioners in their annual report for 1971 prefaced an account of the Sanctuary affair thus:

"Although this is by no means a large charity, we think that the results of our inquiry into it, and the steps that we took subsequently, are of general interest *because it appears that there are a number of other similar charities that are making appeals to the public without any prospect of their ever being satisfactorily administered.*" (Author's italics.)

Sanctuary was established in November 1968 by a trust deed made by Mr Robert Jones and his sister Mrs Margaret Ebelthite for the relief of distress and suffering among children in the United Kingdom, particularly children born in Britain of Indian or Pakistani descent. Mr Jones effectively controlled the charity. As the result of complaints, the Commissioners opened investigations in January 1971. Here are some of the investigating officers' findings:

Mr Jones began by buying 1,050 collecting boxes but only 596 were ever taken into use and of this number 221 could not be accounted for at the time of the inquiry. Others had been left in public houses or elsewhere and not collected. There was considerable looseness in the system of accounting for collections while 'very high' commissions were paid to people who took round boxes. Mr Jones said they were usually ten per cent, sometimes 15 per cent and, on rare occasions, up to 25 per cent. But the report showed that some regular commissions went up to 35 per cent and one collector got 50 per cent, apparently on behalf of a commercial charity-collecting office that he ran.

The Commissioners' report continued:

> The accounts for the period from the setting up of the charity in the summer of 1968 to December 31, 1970 (the last date for which audited accounts were available at the time of the report) showed that about £5,700 had been contributed by the public, although undoubtedly there were other sums in addition that had never been recorded in the accounts. Out of this, only a few hundred pounds had been set aside at the time of the report to accumulate for the ultimate use for charitable purposes. Not a penny had been actually spent on relieving suffering of any child. The rest of the money had been spent on administrative and fund-raising expenses, many of which were unnecessarily extravagant.

Understandably, the Commissioners decided that the trustees had been guilty of misconduct and mis-management. They 'froze' the charity's bank account, removed Mr Jones and his sister as trustees, and appointed the National Society for the Prevention of Cruelty to Children in their place. Mr

Jones appealed to the High Court, where it was thrown out, the judge commenting: " . . . Mr Jones simply is not suitable to be a trustee of the charity. Mr Jones has from time to time in the course of presenting his case cast serious aspersions on the Charity Commissioners and others. I have fully appreciated the stress to which he has been subject but the least I can do is to make it perfectly clear that such aspersions are quite unjustifiable."

The Commissioners ended their report on the Sanctuary case with this warning:

> We think we should draw attention to the need for members of the public who put their money into collecting boxes presented to them in such places as public houses and supermarkets to satisfy themselves about the use that will be made of the money. Unless the name of the charity appearing on the collecting box is that of a well-known and reputable charity, it is as well, before contributing, to inquire whether the collector receives any commissions on what he collects and if so how much, and also to ask what the charity has actually achieved with the money which it receives.

During their inquiries into the Sanctuary charity, the Commissioners learned of an organization set up by 'a person with known criminal antecedents', which purported to collect funds for charity. Investigations and a formal inquiry under Section 6 of the Charities Act showed that the organization was not in itself a charity and made substantial deductions for non-charitable purposes from sums collected while the principal organizer purported also to act as one of the trustees of a certain charity. It was discovered that the fund-raising organization remitted only a fraction of the sums collected on behalf of a North Midlands charity and that deductions were made for commissions for collectors and the organizer as well as office salaries.

"It seems clear," the Commissioners commented, "that the trustees of the North Midland charity had taken inadequate steps to prevent the public from being misled about the proportion of the money collected which would actually go to the charity. The arrangements with the non-charitable fund-raising organization have since been terminated by the (North Midland) charity and one of the trustees has resigned. . . ."

The Commissioners can bite when necessary!

11

'LITTLE FOR PUBLIC DISQUIET'

There are something like 4,000 local organizations devoted to voluntary social service in Britain, most of them area branches of national organizations and most of them also 'charities' by virtue of their work – a voluntary social service may be described as the organization and activities of a self-governing body of people who have joined together voluntarily to study or act for the betterment of the community.

Before World War I, through it all and immediately after, the number of such organizations and of straightforward money-giving charities had grown enormously and the need was seen for some co-ordination of effort and prevention, or at least containment, of overlapping. The National Council of Social Service was established in 1919, broadly to act as middleman between central Government and local social service organizations, presenting united views on proposed legislation for example, and overseeing many quasi-Government organizations. The Council, for instance, runs the Citizens Advice Bureaux to be found throughout the country, organizes local councils of Social Service and, since 1924, has had its own Charities Aid Fund which provides a direct method of charity-giving and also a specialist service to companies and trusts in the administration of their donations. The fund receives money – subscriptions, donations, legacies – in the same way as any single charity and distributes it either at its own discretion or in accordance with the wishes of the original donor if any are expressed. In this way the fund distributes about £2m a year to charities.

The National Council co-ordinates the work of about 130 'national' charities and over the years has accumulated a vast fund of experience, which was one of the reasons why it was the body asked by the Charity Commissioners to set up a working party to examine all aspects of charity fund-raising and consider the possibility of a 'code of conduct' for fund-raising.

The Charity Commissioners are mainly concerned with the manner in which charities *spend* money, they are not required to investigate fund-raising methods. But they received complaints that, for instance, too small a proportion of money donated went to charitable work, that some fund-raising methods were distasteful or liable to damage the general image of charity work. The working party was set up in January 1958 and consisted of executives of some of the largest charities, officials of the National Council of Social Service, a solicitor, an accountant, and other specialists in the field, including public relations and advertising men. Their final report was lengthy, comprehensive and searching.

The working party did not probe criminal activities in the charity world nor did they deal with allegations that some charities were run exclusively for the benefit of the organizers, commenting: "We were ready to receive evidence . . . but not a single case of this kind was brought before us . . . We have no evidence of any registered charity being exploited for the benefit of those in charge of it." (That may have been the case at the time, but consider the implications of some of the Charity Commissioners's reports since!)

The investigation began with 356 complaints made to the Charity Commissioners between 1 January 1963 and 26 April 1968. The Commissioners gave evidence that about 100 complaints concerned charity advertising, 19 concerned professional fund-raisers, 64 concerned fund-raising methods, and 21 concerned the high costs of appeals or doubt as to whether the contributions all reached the beneficiaries. There were 17 complaints about the organization of competitions, 39 about second-hand clothes, 39 about charity shops and 57 about football pools. Of all the complaints, 182 came from the general public, 20 from the police, 12 from Members of Parliament, 11 from the Government or local authorities, 39 from other charities, eight from former charity employees, 46 from the Press, and 38 from the Charity Commissioners themselves. Complaints covered such aspects as the cost of advertising, the accuracy of appeals, high-pressure techniques forced on some charities by the activities of others, payment of collectors, unsolicited gifts through the post and associated appeal methods, poor organization of competitions, the honesty of clothing-collection contractors, and the percentage shops gave to charity.

Everything was done by the working party to gather criticism – they even advertised for it – but they got only six replies. They investigated casual criticial remarks but could get no factual evidence here at all and commented that there was some evidence that people who had a guilty feeling about not doing much for charity and people who gave nothing at all sometimes gave reasons which were 'mere rationalization', in other words they engaged in generalized attacks, a habit which can do a great deal of damage to charities. On fund-raising then, the working party reported:

> Having searched diligently and with open minds, we are bound to report that the volume of complaint which we have been able to unearth is insignificant in relation to the size of charitable operations, and we believe that on the whole the public have few specific criticisms about fund-raising for charity which they are able to substantiate. As the Chartered Institute of Secretaries said: "There does not seem to be any notable concern at the fund-raising activities of charities . . . Particular criticism of individual charities, on the other hand, is a hazard which is well known to non-profit making bodies, whether charities, professional societies or trade organizations, who lack the yard-stick of profitability and who success can be measured only in imprecise terms if at all. Criticism of this kind should be accepted as a fact of life and as a means of ensuring that the activities of an organization are periodically subject to close scrutiny by supporters."
>
> *Having made it clear that we found very little which should cause any public disquiet about the conduct of charities, we are far from saying that there is no room for improvement. There are many questions to be faced in connection with fund-raising, and far too little is known both by the general public and by charities themselves about some of these questions.*

The working party gave its own answer to the repeated questions 'Are fund-raising charities necessary? Should they not all be taken over by the Government?' Said the report:

> Most charities would agree that the Government might well give further aid to various charitable needs but the simple fact is that most of the work which charitable funds finance just would not be done if it was left to the Government to do it . . . Various fields of work have been, with the full consent of the charities concerned, taken over by the State as the need is recognized to be the responsibility of every tax-payer and too large to be supported by charitable giving. For example, school milk and school meals, the legal aid scheme, hospital social work and many other innovations were all pioneered by voluntary organizations and have since been taken over by the State. Charities are more free to undertake experiments than a statutory authority; they can risk failure . . .

When it came to studying administration and fund-raising expenses and the accounts of charities, the working party made a number of valuable points. They found, for instance, that analysis of charity accounts did not disclose excessive administration expenses, as distinct from fund-raising costs, largely because many accounts do not distinguish them clearly enough. The working party received criticisms of glossy publications, showy annual reports, expensive headquarters and so on and there was a tendency to approve more of charities using voluntary staff services and inexpensive staff. It is accepted that salaries are mostly below commercial levels, particularly for administrative grades, but it is pointed out that there are limits to what can be done cheaply and limits also on the discipline and control which can be exerted over voluntary workers. Then, the cost of bad or indifferent administration by the underpaid may be far heavier than getting the best person for the job.

The report expressed the belief that charities should not hesitate to engage staff at realistic salaries and pointed out that professional staff such as nurses and teachers had to be paid at agreed national rates. "We found," they added, "that one of the reasons why some charities are forced to go to the expense of permanently employing outside consultants is because paying the market rate for a similar person to be a member of the staff would throw out of gear the charity's own salary structure."

There is the argument that it is not wise to attempt to administer a charity from unattractive and inefficient offices – most businesses know the value of good working conditions. "We think that the vague allegations of over-spending on salaries and other things intended to produce good work are mis-directed and may in fact cause waste."

Dealing with the frequent allegation that some charities are 'well-meaning but woolly' – something on which practically everyone dealing with charity agrees is still true to a certain extent – the report quotes the National Institute for the Blind: "This concept may at one time have been justified but there is no excuse for it today. The public is entitled to expect – and be shown that it is getting – a high standard of professional competence in the charities which appeal to it – a professional competence which nevertheless does not obscure or over-ride the principles of sympathy and understanding and concern for the individual which are the very foundations of all charitable effort."

Saying that all charities should be encouraged to show 'administration' or 'administration expenses' as a separate heading in their accounts – as many now do – the report deals with the difficulty of determining what should come under such heads. "Our view is that administration expenses are those of central management and organization of the society's affairs, secretariat, accounting, etc., other activities at headquarters being classed as services in connection with the prime object of the society or as fund-raising." But there can be problems for small charities with a minimal staff, where an official may be both a welfare worker and an administrator or where much of the welfare work is also of an administrative nature. Noting that some charities do disclose administrative costs in a readily understandable manner and that an element of competition in claiming cheap administration existed, the report records what happened when Oxfam wrote to the *Sunday Telegraph* in June 1968, showing how each half-crown of revenue was spent, including a penny-farthing for administration, such as salaries, telephone bills and so on. Promptly a reader wrote in to the paper, pointing out that a penny-farthing out of half a crown as a proportion of the gross annual income of Oxfam of £3m (at that time) represented £125,000 per annum, or £2,400 per week – "which, when one gains the impression that much of their labour is voluntary, seems a lot of money."

The report says flatly: "It is impossible, and would be inappropriate, to lay down any fixed percentage of income which should be the limit for administration expenses. The performance of each charity in this respect must be judged individually in the light of the type of service which it provides."

Discussing fund-raising costs, the working party recorded some charities as reportedly willing to spend up to one-third of their revenue on fund-raising, one view that the limit should be ten per cent, and the fact that the Winston Churchill Memorial Appeal raised nearly £3m at an overall expense figure of only 2.6 per cent. Other charity fund-raising expense figures quoted are Dr Barnardo's 15 per cent, Oxfam 12 per cent, and the Royal National Institute for the Blind 17 per cent (all figures at the time of the report, it should be noted). It was pointed out that new charities and those dealing with unpopular causes have higher fund-raising expenses. Ways of raising money differ. House collections cost less per £1 raised than a charity ball. It is more expensive if first a charity has to educate the public on the need for support of a particular cause. Then again, expense ratios rise in time of economic stress, when the public are less able or willing to give.

Several large national charities told the working party that, assuming local committee expenses had been deducted at source, the fund-raising cost to headquarters, including advertising, national appeals and so on need not normally exceed 15 per cent. One big fund-raising company gave evidence that between September 1959 and June 1968 it raised more than £27m for clients at a total outlay (including fees and expenses) of five per cent. The company added that it would be unhappy if costs rose above 15 per cent and preferred to keep them at ten per cent.

Other matters investigated by the working party are dealt with in various chapters of this book, but here is a summary of some of their conclusions.

The number of complaints about charities is notably small – few facts have emerged; there is very little to cause public disquiet but the public and charities themselves should be better informed on many problems.

Administrative costs should be shown separately, but these are difficult to define and it is not possible or right to lay down a fixed upper limit for such expenses.

There should be more guidance on the presentation of accounts and perhaps a special study involving accounts and auditors to produce a guide of the type available in the United States and Canada.

There is a need for more legislation to deal with misleading or deceptive claims by 'non-charities' as a result of which registered charities suffer.

The rules relating to advertising standards should be applied to charity advertising at least as strictly as to commercial advertising.

Further efforts should be made to avoid the overlapping of appeals. Unification of collections might be applied to a few groups of charities.

On balance there should be a code of conduct for fund-raising but it would not be desirable for this to be legally enforceable. It should have the voluntary acceptance of as wide a range of charities as possible. Both charities and the public should get more guidance on fund-raising philosophy and problems.

One is tempted here to ask: Who is going to do the guiding?

12

THE PROFESSIONAL BEGGARS

One of the most common public criticisms of charitable activity, largely uninformed, is directed at the professional fund-raisers. This is partly a reflection of the feeling, already mentioned, that nobody should make money for themselves in any way out of charity work, even draw wages or salaries, but also of a widespread suspicion that this is the area where most of 'the rackets' take place!

Most of the very big charities themselves quite openly sneer at fund-raising companies. "We do not employ professional fund-raisers" is the cold comment and, if asked why not, they assert that fund-raising companies know nothing about the work of 'our' charity, and add "We can do it just as well ourselves." One argument used here is that it is preferable for a charity with sufficient popular appeal to go for the pennies of the poor rather than the millionaire's £5,000 donation. "Twenty 5ps are better than a pound note", one of the most successful charity administrators is fond of saying. "You have a broad base from which to collect, it is less likely to dry up – as can happen with a small number of generous donors, who may become poorer and, in any event, will die sooner or later."

There *have* been a few cases in the last ten years or so, to take just that period, of crooked fund-raising companies, or at least 'greedy' ones. But they have been extremely rare, most were one-man shows and most, if not all, have been wiped out by adverse publicity. It can be said with confidence that the large fund-raising companies in Britain are above reproach and very, very efficient.

The National Council of Social Service working party discussed professional companies in detail. Taking first charity 'function' organizers, the people who arrange the glamorous balls, the galas and celebrity concerts, the report commented: "To a charity which has not the necessary information or contacts or which has not got the staff for the operation, the services of the right person for a special occasion are indispensable for its success, and the feeling that there is something improper in receiving a fee for these services is a hangover from the days when life in the charitable world was a great deal more leisurely." But the report added: "As regards the professional fund-raisers, however, much more needs to be known."

Professional fund-raisers, reported the working party, are principally involved in university, school and other educational projects, church and cathedral appeals, special campaigns for charities and capital-raising ventures generally, usually where there is a 'captive constituency' and where appeals to the general public are not involved. They tend to specialize even within these fields, leaving for example one firm to handle most of the preparatory school appeals. The report continues:

> There is no doubt that the fund-raisers set out to maintain the highest professional standards in their work. Broadly speaking the procedure adopted is to survey the prospects of a possible campaign, including the target to be aimed at, to select a suitable campaign director from their list (which contains a large number of retired Service officers), to ascertain the 'constituency' to be approached, prepare the literature and programme, and see that it is carried out, possibly with a follow-up at a later date. Often a campaign is directed to obtaining seven-year covenants. It could be said that in many cases one is paying an organization such as this to drive one to do what one could mostly do for oneself if one had the confidence and determination, but that perhaps does not matter if it is in fact the only way of getting the result.

Observing that many campaigns have been smoothly carried through, the report went on:

> But there have been failures about which it is not so easy to obtain information. It has been reported that there are some results which do not come up to expectation in a number of cases. The Countess of Mar and Kelly was reported as being disappointed with the appeal for Carberry Tower, a church centre near Musselburgh, which was to raise £75,000 through professional fund-raisers but achieved only £8,000. The appeal for £75,000 to commemorate Sir Edward Appleton had after a year raised only about £12,000. The campaign by the North Eastern Association for the Arts to raise £500,000 over seven years had after a year cost £17,000 and produced £35,000 with promises bringing the total to £41,000; the fund-raisers' agreement was for one year at a fee of £13,500 with

> £5,000 in local administrative expenses. We have no doubt that explanations could be given in all these cases and that the failure, if failure it be, would not always turn out to be that of the fund-raisers. It does point, however, to the fact that considerable judgement is needed on the part of the charity as well as the professional firm before entering into a commitment.

Referring to 19 criticisms of professional fund-raisers listed for the working party by the Charity Commissioners, the report noted that if a campaign failed it could happen that all donations could go to the professional firm and it might even be necessary to draw on other funds of a charity to pay the fees and expenses.

> This leads naturally to the suggestion that the professional firms ought to work on a percentage of results. Very few of them will do, or would agree that it is ethical. It is of course in line with the practice of most professionals to charge for work done irrespective of success and, although we have questioned whether this is necessarily right in the case of fund-raisers, and although we are not impressed with all the arguments which have been advanced in support of it, we think it must be left to them to decide the basis on which they will work.

Working on a percentage basis, a firm – which has its own overheads to carry – might well allow a margin for risk which would make the final fee higher.

The working party concluded:

> We cannot ignore the fact that the professional firm is in the best position to assess the risk involved in embarking on a campaign and one consultant has suggested that in most cases it could be a required condition of employment that, if the cost of the exercise exceeds a certain percentage, the excess cost should be borne by the consultant rather than by the charity. We think the safeguard fairest to both sides would be for it to become accepted practice to insert in all contracts a break clause giving either side the right to terminate the campaign after a trial period, which might be three or possibly six months.

A point made in one of the Charity Commission reports is that when a charity does employ a professional fund-raising company, either on commission or for a flat fee, the charity's accounts may only show the net revenue raised.

There can certainly be a big disparity between the total

amount given to a campaign and the net result. The major charities generally operate on anything between about ten and 33 per cent of all revenue to cover their total expenses, including fund-raising, and this has been compared with 50 per cent overheads at an average grocery shop and 20 per cent or so at the cheapest supermarket.

Some one-man or small professional fund-raising companies have been reported as charging 50 per cent commission, others 30 per cent – but nobody will name names or admit to ever having paid out such proportions. One of the largest companies, which raised millions of pounds, claims that its total fees and expenses work out at about five per cent per project. It should be pointed out, however, that these major companies deal mainly with the 'captive' donors.

The December 1973 issue of the consumer magazine *Money Which*, surveying the costs of 36 leading charities, largely through 1972, showed that fund-raising costs ranged from a massive 26.3 per cent for the British and Foreign Bible Society down to 1.8 per cent for the Imperial Cancer Research Fund. The British Legion fund-raising costs were 24.3 per cent, including the cost of poppies and wreaths, and Shelter 22.6 per cent. An interesting comparison is that Dr Barnardo's fund-raising costs were 12.1 per cent and those of Help the Aged 12.8 while the administration costs were 3.5 per cent for the huge Barnardo organization but 3.9 per cent for the infinitely smaller Help the Aged. The administration costs of other charities included 33.4 per cent for the British Diabetic Association, 26.9 per cent for the British Red Cross Society and 14.7 per cent for the British Legion. The Cancer Research Campaign figure, however, was only 1.5 per cent and that for the Royal National Institute for the Blind 1.1 per cent.

Money Which concluded that on average the fund-raising costs of the 36 charities came to 11.5 per cent. On the figures published by the magazine, administration costs averaged 8.2 per cent.

Big-time professional charity fund-raising really started in Britain in 1955, with the arrival from the United States of Colonel Wells. In a few years he and his organization tripled the income of about 1,000 British charities. His son Frank, now chairman of the organization, talks bluntly about the whole business:

> Large fund-raising is extremely intensive. Fund-raising in Britain is different from anywhere else in the world. In many charities the

right hand doesn't know what the left hand is doing. People who have worked for charity for 15 or 20 years at a low salary are dedicated, sure, but they get less and less efficient. Some governing bodies consist of people who think they're doing a favour by allowing their names to be used . . . but they are personally the non-givers! Many charities advocate the broad-base approach, a great number of small donations, but that can take five to ten years to organize. I prefer to get the money from one person or a few, then move on to widespread collection if necessary.

We work for a flat fee, not on commission. Commission puts the givers off, especially the big ones – imagine what a man would say if he knew that 15 per cent of his £10,000 donation was going in commission! We won't take on the impossible. Whatever the cause, a university, a professional body, a church or even a whole diocese, we first have a planning study. In most cases charities come to us to help them raise money on the basis of what they think they can get away with at the immediate moment, not considering the position five to ten years hence. Even the sophisticated don't do their homework properly.

A planning study can cost as little as £75 but £750 to £1,500 flat fee is a typical sort of thing. The idea is to develop a financial programme, determining the needs over a five to ten-year period. Then we look at the sources of funds, including alternatives which perhaps the charity never thought of. For example, if a public school has surplus funds, some of these may be used – why should the parents or old boys have to pay fully for a new building? We can set up voluntary bodies to do the collecting when properly briefed. There is one major rule – *don't necessarily give the client what he wants!* I'm told that £100,000 is required. Will less do? Or is the figure high enough? Perhaps fund-raising can be spread over more time if the cause is the type that can be financed over a period.

In our field the bulk of donations come from a few big givers. The top ten donations can often represent 25 to 50 per cent of the total raised. In one campaign we raised £5m from 300 donors and 86 per cent of the total came from one-third of the donors. The most efficient way of raising money is from *one* source! As for the objection that professional fund-raisers do not understand a charity's problems, well they all say that – and it's not true. What we bring is a professional detachment to the problem. You know, the churches in particular just hate the idea of paying flat fees for fund-raising!

One man who has raised money for charity is not at all keen on doing it again. Says Jeffrey Archer, the man who organized the famous charity show at the Royal Festival Hall on behalf of the United World Colleges (formerly 'Atlantic

Colleges'): "I won't generally take on charity work, it's unremunerative. I'm basically a show business promotor." Archer put Frank Sinatra and Princess Grace of Monaco on for two shows at the Festival Hall in one day. A Sunday newspaper afterwards reported that £150,000 was raised, adding "The real winner that night seemed to have been Mr Jeffery Archer M.P. The stars gave their services free but Mr Archer, whose firm organized the show, is reported to have made £8,000 out of it."

The facts? "Well, we sold 1,000 seats at £50 each and all in all we grossed £750,000 in the United Kingdom alone from various rights, and overseas TV rights brought in something like another £500,000. We made a net profit for ourselves of only £2,000 – because it took nearly a year's organizing work. You know, if fund-raisers are supposed to know little about charity work, none of the charities know anything about running shows!"

Mr Archer says that quite a number of the millionaires who are approached for help may decline. "They get so many demands these days", he said. "A known millionaire probably gets about a hundred begging letters a week. I myself get around 50. Personally I'm giving £10,000 this year to charity, but I give only to about half a dozen organizations, very much of my own personal choice."

That Festival Hall concert was, of course, one of the all-time top successes. Then there was the Royal Gala Cabaret staged at London's Talk of the Town for the World Wildlife Fund, of which the Duke of Edinburgh is president. This was fund-raising on the grand scale. Led by the Queen, it was attended by 17 other members of British and European Royal families: the Duke of Edinburgh, Prince Charles, Princess Anne, Princess Alexandra, Queen Juliana of the Netherlands, her husband, Prince Bernhard and daughter Princess Beatrix, King Constantine and Queen Anne-Marie of The Hellenes, the Grand Duke and Grand Duchess of Luxembourg, the Crown Prince and Crown Princess of Norway, the Crown Princess of Denmark and her husband Prince Henrik, the Prince of Liege, brother of King Baudouin of Belgium, and Prince Don Carlos of Spain, nephew of the Spanish Pretender.

With a turn-out like that perhaps the artists were of slightly lesser importance than usual! But they were: Glen Campbell, Petula Clark, Rex Harrison, Bob Hope, Engelbert Humperdinck, Tom Jones, George Kirby, Millicent Martin, Rudolph Nureyev and Antoinette Sibley. In addition to the orchestras there were also the State Trumpeters of the Life Guards. The World Wildlife Fund made a profit "in excess of £125,000" but said, "It would be misleading to discuss the gross revenue and expenses of an individual event like this because, of course, the ratios do vary very much from one event to another and it is the overall performance of a charity that is important, not necessarily the particular ratio of an individual event."

That statement reflects the attitude of most charities to the cost and profit of their big fund-raising events. Few appear to be prepared to be totally revealing. Some do not want to disclose their expertise, or lack of it. With certain exceptions the big charities take the view that the grand balls of the past are too expensive to stage today and produce too little money at the end of it all. One reason often cited is that there are not enough big houses left in London where such affairs can be staged (but see Chapter 21 for how the Distressed Gentlefolks Aid Association gets over this problem). Nevertheless a considerable sum of money is raised through what the charities freely admit is straight 'snob appeal'. Probably only the Duke of Edinburgh could round up 17 'royals' – other charities are delighted when they can get one. The two most famous organizers of such events are undoubtedly Mrs Madge Clarke and Miss Irene Edwards. Both of them have talked frankly about their work.

Mrs Clarke confirms that charity balls are expensive. In March 1973 she gave these figures for the Air Ball at London's Dorchester Hotel: cost of dinner £3 per head, including ballroom; the 500 or so guests paid £4.50 each and about £800 net came from the meal; tombola raised £225, programme sales £106, a draw £87; printing cost £512, secretarial help £119, advertising £23, postage, stationery and telephone £58.37, and accountant's fee £31.50. Two bands cost a total of £144.50 and a discotheque £25. Mrs Clarke charged £300, "just about average for me". Not an immense sum could have been left for charity.

Mrs Clarke has gone on record as saying that the greatest attraction for a charitable function is the presence of the Queen Mother, followed by the Queen, Princess Alexandra, Princess Anne and the Duchess of Kent.

Miss Edwards once raised £143,000 in a single evening for the British Hertford Hospital in Paris by organizing a reception at St James's Palace attended by the Queen Mother and two other 'royals'. Cash returns are different now. The Invalid Children's Aid Association, for whom Miss Edwards organized a charity stage show, netted about £10,000. They had to pay £2,500 for the theatre but got £5,000 from advertisements in the programme. Seats cost between £1.50 and £25. Miss Edwards arranges about six or seven functions like this each year at a fee of up to £500 each. Nobody knows better than she how to get the best value out of the rich. She was quoted as saying: "Today there are many more rich people but so many of them give only for what they can get. They try to bully or wheedle you into giving them places near royalty . . . You've no idea what I'd be offered for an *introduction* to a royal!" She says the young people of today aren't interested in the old-style charity ball – "They'd prefer an evening in a creepy barn, smoking pot!"

But a country house ball can still pull in the money. Miss Edwards once asked millionaire Paul Getty to lend his home, Sutton Place. She submitted a list of 100 millionaires to the Queen Mother's Lady-in-Waiting. Sixty were invited to dinner with the Queen Mother and Mr Getty at Sutton Place, and Yehudi Menuhin was to play afterwards. The result was about £10,000 for the Central Council for the Disabled.

That's the way it's done if you are a skilful organizer. Though such a professional, Miss Edwards has, by the way, a typical British charity weakness. "I never, never charge an *animal* charity. I try to do at least one function a year for nothing."

Some 'non-professionals' are also very efficient. Mrs Sheila Rawsthorne, of the Stars Organization for Spastics, organized a world premier of the film *Nicholas and Alexandra* for the Spastic Society, attended by Princess Anne. The theatre and the film were provided free – which is unusual these days – and Mr and Mrs J. Edward Sieff gave a party to launch the performance. Mr Louis Roederer donated champagne, Dunhill sent cigarettes. Honorary Treasurer Mr Leslie Grade saw to it that every expense was underwritten by somebody. The Spastics Society got about £70,000.

13

SUSPICIONS, RACKETS, AND TRADING

Football pools, flag days, and door-to-door collections of money or clothing form important sources of revenue for some registered charities and, as we have seen, all three methods have been attacked. Pools raise about £6m a year for charity but nobody knows whether this will continue to be the case. In 1971 a special act was passed permitting charities to continue to operate betting lotteries for five years, pending a Government investigation into the whole law on lotteries. Two big charities relying heavily on pools have been the Spastics Society and the National Fund for Research into Crippling Diseases. The Director of the National Fund, Mr Duncan Guthrie, prepared a special report for the National Council of Social Service working party on charitable fund-raising, in which he said that the two main pools organizations raising money for charity had produced more than £20m. In its own report the working party commented that 'a considerable section of the public' deplores the use of gambling to raise money for charity.

The complaints and the criticisms largely concern small pool operators whose contribution to charity is sometimes questionable and whose business efficiency may be even more so. Said the working party:

> Complaints in the case of one football pool alleged that the request for a voluntary donation of a penny-halfpenny per week was hidden in the small print while the charitable object was given overwhelming prominence in large print and the literature was distributed by children from door to door. It was also alleged that most people believed that the operation was largely or wholly in aid of the charities, reinforced by representations on the doorstep, and that the promotional methods were designed to foster this impression. There are also instances alleged by the Press of pools being promoted which are improperly conducted. There is not much substance in these allegations in those cases where registered charities are involved, but charities should try to ensure that the

pools in which they are interested should not be conducted in such a way as to give substance to those allegations.

Referring to pools not specifically linked to the name of a particular registered charity, but using vague terms such as 'for kidney disease' or 'for cancer', the report warned that people should not give for any charitable cause unless the collector can produce good evidence of his *bona fides*.

It is all very well for the National Council, and the Charity Commissioners for that matter, to issue this warning. But in practice most people are far too shy to challenge collectors, to appear to be casting doubts on their honesty, especially in a public place. One way round this constant problem might be to make it compulsory for all collectors to wear, when working, a badge issued by the charitable organization for which the money is asked. The absence of such a badge would be simple to challenge. "Where's your badge?" is an easy question to ask.

For all these pools, the tickets should show clearly the name or names of the charities involved and the exact amount per ticket that is going to charity. Small pools, operated in association with parish churches for instance, can be shockingly badly administered, even though with honest intent. One such pool that once operated in a number of London suburbs carried on for months *unknowingly* paying out to churches each week more than it actually took in. A mistake on the right side perhaps, but indicative of what can happen.

Door-to-door collections, as we have seen, are inclined to cause more public ire than almost anything else, for the reason that they make it much more difficult to refuse to give money. The antagonism thus produced is not concentrated solely on the charities engaging in such methods, it is spread across the whole field. Most particularly disliked is the door-to-door envelope collection, largely because the money given here is a form of conscience money; people give to get the collector away from the door and permit them to get back to the TV or their guests or whatever. Irritation is caused also when envelopes are left but not collected later, and this happens quite often – probably because the home was empty when the collector called the second time. The report on attitudes to charity quoted in Chapter 2 pointed out that people knowing that it is right to give to charity feel that they will be seen as both misers and misanthropes if they refuse to give when asked eye-to-eye. They complain that they can't help everybody, yet it is doubtful whether the average household is directly importuned for money more than once a month.

There is a lot of suspicion of door-to-door collection for lesser-known charities, worthy as they may be. The more belligerent householder may raise questions on the doorstep, but not many do. Apart from not demanding identification, people are very unlikely to ask point-blank the question at the back of many minds: "How much commission do *you* get?" Most charities deny that they pay commission to door-to-door collectors but at least one major charity executive supports the idea because, he says, it keeps collectors honest! He has a point here, for in some cases there is little or nothing to prevent a dishonest collector from milking the box, whereas if he gets a commission, the more money he turns in the larger his cut will be. And with those charities reported as paying 33⅓ per cent commission the sum could be well worth earning.

It is easy to satisfy oneself that door-to-door collectors are who they purport to be, given the nerve to challenge. Such collections for *any* charitable purpose constitute an offence unless licensed by the local police, who must be satisfied that the amount of money likely to go to the charity concerned is sufficient in relation to the total collected. The charity applying for such permission must prevent unauthorized persons obtaining prescribed badges or certificates, must ensure that collectors are of good character, and is responsible for any contravention by the collectors of the House to House Collections Act 1939. We have already noted that some charitable collections on a national scale may be exempted from police control by the Home Secretary. From the charities' point of view, door-to-door collections cost considerably less than many other fund-raising methods, such as staging a ball or a concert, particularly if all the collectors are unpaid.

Door-to-door collections of clothing for charity raise a number of doubts and criticisms. Here the suspicion is that many collectors really are just 'rag and bone' men and that the clothing will never find its way to any charitable institution. There are a number of people who push cards and paper sacks through letter boxes, stating that 'Mr X.Y.Z. will call tomorrow and will be grateful for old clothing, etc. He gives money to charity weekly', or some such phraseology. Beware of these! Neither the amount of money given or the name of the charity is disclosed. But it is remarkable how many people fall for this racket. The National Council of Social Service report in the section dealing with gifts in kind – which may include a wide range of things – said: "Charities should state as precisely as practicable the kind and quality of gifts required, the purposes for which they are needed, and how they will be disposed of. In the case of clothing, particular care should be taken by the appeal to describe what is and what is not asked for or required." Noting the number of cricitisms of clothing collections referred to them by the Charity Commissioners which questioned the honesty or the methods of contractors and the lack of control over them by charities, the working party recommended tight supervision by charities and added: "Charities collecting waste clothing and other things through agencies should note the advice given by the Waste Trade Federation as follows: 'It is inadvisable for any charity to license rag merchants or others to collect materials in the name of a charity, accounting only to the charity for a contracted sum or a percentage. There is no reason at all why the public should not be encouraged to give unwanted materials to a charity but we feel that if the charity wants to get the full value of the gift they should contract to sell the goods so collected by auction or tender to a merchant or merchants whom we could suggest.' "

A very suspect phrase indeed, sometimes seen on the side of tradesmen's vans, is 'for the general welfare of the blind', or the disabled, or something similar. These are simply commercial trading concerns selling a variety of goods such as brushes and brooms, for instance, which they suggest are made by the blind or handicapped people – or there may be the implication that charity benefits if you buy from them. The eminently respectable Remploy organization has had to complain of many imitators, of people trading falsely on its image.

A number of such concerns are one-man operations but by no means all. There is still nothing like the control over charity trading companies as over registered charities and there have been a number of cases of firms using charitable-sounding names to mislead the public. It was estimated in 1972 that there were about 40 such firms in existence throughout the country. When Mr David Reed M.P. was presenting in the House of Commons his Trading Representation (Disabled Persons) Amendment Bill (which was unopposed) he said that racketeering firms employed disabled people for small wages "and the bumper profits on shoddy goods go to the directors, the organization and the schoolboy student sales force." All over the country householders were being taken for a ride. Mr Reed added that one estimate suggested something like £1m was going into the wrong hands. Goods were often manufacturers' rejects or end-of-production runs which would not sell on their own merits. He cited one firm which to indicate its interest in the disabled had one disabled person, with a £1 share, in the company. He revealed, too, that some such firms hire out certificates under the Trading Registration (Disabled Persons) Act 1958 from one concern to another on a day-to-day basis!

These companies, and the one-man shows, use many devices to suggest respectability, while at the same time generally being very careful about the phraseology they employ. Typical is something like this: 'The X.Y.Z. Charity Collecting Company, registered under the Registration of Business Names Act 1916'. This means little of course and should alert most people.

There was a classic case of a company which sold articles from door to door at about seven times the wholesale price, saying the proceeds were for a certain – genuine – charity. That charity received only about 16 per cent of the profits. 'Borrowing' of charity names by quite unauthorised people can be a serious worry for some charities, especially the more popular ones. For example, on one occasion somebody even had Royal National Lifeboat Institution notepaper printed.

A number of charities enter into arrangements with commercial firms which are both legitimate and highly profitable. There is the system whereby, for giving their seal of approval to a certain item, a charity receives a royalty on sales. This is looked upon with disfavour in some quarters, one reason being that the charity is normally in no position to guarantee the quality of the goods which they have 'approved'. Much better are joint schemes such as those that have been used by the Royal National Lifeboat Institution and the Royal Society for the Prevention of Cruelty to Animals, both forceful fund-raisers. Birds Eye and the R.N.L.I. worked out a promotion under which people were asked to return to the company a token with the nominal value of 6d on packets of fish fingers over a nine-week summer period. Birds Eye offered to pay the R.N.L.I. the value of the returned tokens or £30,000, whichever was the greater, to go to the cost of a lifeboat. Fish finger sales soared, the promotion was repeated, and the R.N.L.I. got £60,000 in all. A somewhat similar arrangement was made between the R.S.P.C.A. and Mars Petfoods. The result was that the society received £80,000 of free television advertising, increased its membership by more than 16,000, and got £39,100 raised by the public taking part in the promotion. Reported the R.S.P.C.A. "It was widely claimed as one of the most successful commercial/charity promotions ever to have been run."

Commenting in its fund-raising report on overheads involved in some forms of association between charities and commercial concerns, the National Council for Social Service said that with some such arrangements expenses will be relatively high and sometimes even 50 per cent of the gross takings from the public is considered too low. They noted that in small lotteries only 40 per cent of the stake money had to go to charity while only between eight and 16 per cent of the money paid in by the public to football pools usually went to the charitable purpose concerned. The report recommended: "Where arrangements with commercial firms preclude the percentage of gross takings which will accrue to the charity concerned being stated in advance in the promotional literature, charities should take all possible steps to ensure that expenses should not exceed a maximum of 50 per cent of the gross takings except in unusual and explainable circumstances."

With the continuing uncertainty about the future of football pools and governmental intentions, some charities that for years relied heavily on pools have moved increasingly into the general trading business, accompanied by others simply wishing to expand their revenues. Trading companies of differing proportions are operated by, among others, the World Wildlife Fund, Dr Barnardo's, Shelter, the Royal Society for the Protection of Birds, the Scouts and Guides, and the R.S.P.C.A. Oxfam's 300 shops throughout the country are the best-known example in a field in which charities see a promising future. Oxfam told the National Council for Social Service that they expected to get from the shops a yield of five to one, that is a maximum expenditure on overheads of 20 per cent of gross takings. That maximum, however, might be exceeded if goods had to be bought for re-sale supplement gifts.

A charity is not taxable on trading profits if such profits are applied exclusively to the purposes of the charity and either the trade is exercised in the course of carrying out the primary purpose of the charity, or the work in connection with the trade is mainly done by beneficiaries of the charity.

Where neither of these conditions apply – for example Christmas card sales – a charity may be taxable on profits, so the usual practice is to set up a trading company, covenant the profits to the charity involved, and reclaim the tax.

Christmas card sales for charity are now an enormous business, but there have been acute problems. Some of the major charities produce their own cards, like Oxfam which can expect to sell around six million during a good Christmas period, and the Spastics Society, which can sell ten million or more. In such cases the charities may make a reasonable profit, possibly up to 40 per cent. But a charity which does not sell directly and works through a third party such as a retail outlet, may well get less than 20 per cent return and some charities have been thoroughly disillusioned. However, there are plenty of charities still moving into the Christmas card business and taking an ever greater share of the market – possibly as much as 20 per cent today. At first the commercial card companies reacted sharply to this invasion of their territory and some of their spokesmen complained that not enough of the profit on charity cards was actually going to charitable causes. Then certain of the commercial companies, operating on the old principle 'If you can't beat 'em, join 'em', moved in themselves, making contracts with charity organizations to manufacture their cards and retail them. Last Christmas one estimate was that more than 180 million charity cards were sold.

Christmas cards have the additional advantage of helping to keep the name of a charity before the public and in some cases people who buy directly from a charity send back donations as well. The Imperial Cancer Research Fund once reported that about 50 per cent of the people who bought their cards sent donations, which in one year reached £5,000.

Of course the steady advance of charities into the general trading arena is being watched extremely closely by firms who see the possibility of their own profits being eroded. There are commercial firms who consider – and they have a point – that charities enjoy rather unfair advantages in that their emotional appeal helps to sell goods that would otherwise be bought elsewhere, and that charity trading overheads are markedly lower when there is a large element of unpaid help concerned in the shops. While competitiveness both with commercial firms and between the charities themselves is bound to grow to some extent, charities should be very careful not to make too many enemies here! A view put by one of Britain's largest trading companies to the

National Council of Social Service was: "We ourselves have never been affected by trading activities carried on by charities but where the activity is carried on solely for purposes of fund-raising we think objection might reasonably be taken by others who have to earn their livings from the same activity. Where the fund-raising is incidental to a social purpose, such as providing occupation for the disabled, no objection could be made."

The Council's fund-raising report dealt also with what is to some people a thoroughly infuriating practice – sending unsolicited goods through the post. Many charities agree that sending unrequested tickets, goods, seals and so on, accompanied by an appeal, just creates resentment. Said the report:

> We agree with this. Certainly no charity should authorize the dispatch to the public of unsolicited goods on sale-or-return. Many charities hold that this prohibition should extend to articles of little or no intrinsic value, such as Christmas seals . . . We accept the fact that if it is made clear that there is no moral obligation to return or pay for the articles or to send a donation there can be no objection. The charity should ensure that there is no 'follow-up' and that no member of the public who fails to respond is applied to a second time in consecutive years.

This, you know, is rather idealistic. No charity is likely to dispatch goods or whatever and say baldly 'you don't have to pay or return them'. It is self-defeating. Secondly it is doubtful whether most charities have the considerable organization that would be required to check on every recipient and ensure there is no 'follow-up'. Once somebody does get on a charity's list he is liable to be there for a long, long time!

However, the fund-raising report went on:

> We firmly believe that the variety of commercial efforts being made by charities today speaks well for their vitality. The serious abuses, where they exist, lie in the area outside the control either of the Charity Commissioners or the charities themselves, i.e. where unscrupulous individuals or businesses promote their activities under a false cloak of charity. Where charities themselves are concerned the chief danger lies in inexperience and possible damage to their goodwill. The public relations of charity are all-important and need always to be weighed against the money which can be made by successful commercial activities. Particularly where trading is concerned it needs to be borne in mind that merely to run too far ahead of public opinion is in itself danger to goodwill.

14

ACCOUNTING FOR IT ALL

Despite improvements (largely forced by public pressure and the admonitions of the Charity Commissioners over the last few years) the accounts of far too many charities are baffling to an unacceptable extent. It can take hours to untangle an artfully prepared set of company accounts and most charities are nothing if not skilful in this area at least. The public relations office of one of the most important charities in the country, which shall stay nameless, asked to explain a point in his organization's annual accounts said apologetically, "Don't ask me . . . I can't understand that myself!"

The whole philosophy behind a lot of charity accounts is that if they are made difficult enough, fewer people will bother to study them in detail and ask what will almost certainly be regarded as impertinent questions! The aim – which *is* understandable – is always to present the best possible face. But for charities this means emphasizing their heavy costs and playing down income, especially from legacies. It is true! There are charities who will say unashamedly that they like to show in their accounts the lowest possible routine cash income in the hope that it will inspire donors to give more. Another, sometimes conflicting, aim is to make the ratio of expenses, most especially the administrative bracket, appear as favourable as possible. There is a 'low admin. expense league' among charities today! There are several, arguable ways of carrying out this exercise and almost all charity accounts will reflect one or more of the tricks of the trade.

Perhaps the most common – indulged in by some very august charities indeed – is to show only 'net income' from sundry fund-raising activities such as balls, concerts and locally organized events. Obviously these activities costs money (we have looked at some of the figures), but one of the difficulties of studying charity finances at all is that it is usually quite impossible to work out how much is given by the public to a particular fund-raising effort in town X and compare it with the amount that reaches headquarters. *With tens of thousands of local units operating in this way for many charities and only making returns of the 'net' proceeds, it can readily be seen that any estimates of the real total initially given to charity could be, almost certainly is, far, far out. It is a startling thought!*

More easy to spot, if you have a taste for accounts, is the bad habit of hiding legacy income so far as possible. It is not too much to say that *most* charities do not look on legacies as 'income' at all, but acts of God . . . "We never know what size of legacies we are going to get and when", they will tell you. "They are entirely fortuitous, we cannot count on them, we have no means of predicting them and budgeting accordingly, and what we have to show our regular supporters 'in the field' is the routine annual income that they have helped to raise and then emphasize the need to raise more to match our expanding needs and the impact of inflation." It is true, up to a point, that if a charity is known to have received a legacy of, say, half a million pounds, regular voluntary workers may be tempted to take life a bit easier for a time. So, legacies are often allocated straight to capital accounts and do not appear in the general income and expenditure account. There is another advantage – but also a snag – in playing about like this with legacy income. With a charity which receives substantial legacies each year, or most years, the income against which administration expenses (the yardstick always under attack) are set may be increased or reduced according to the way in which the legacies are shown in the accounts.

When they are treated as 'capital receipts', working deficits on general account, if they arise, are met from *ad hoc* transfer from capital. This has the double advantage of keeping down the apparent general income and presenting a picture of a struggling charity having to draw on capital reserves. Very neat! If, however, legacies are treated as direct income, they may then be allocated to straight fund-raising receipts – possibly the most honesty way – or to specific projects, or even set against general administration costs. There are many cases, of course, where a legacy is left for a specific purpose and here the charity must abide by the wishes of the donor so far as practicable.

There is another ingenious little practice. When a large cheque or legacy arrives out of the blue, there are charities who will credit it to the accounts entirely in the year of receipt . . . but there are others who may well spread it over a number of years to help equalize the flow of income brought into account from year to year. Put another way, if administration expenses happen to be specially high in a given year, a charity might well decide to allocate the whole of a good-sized legacy to 'administration' and the ratio of expense to revenue will drop sharply. But the converse can happen also. If a charity has a sudden, big drop in legacy income, as happens, the expense ratios – general, fund-raising or administrative – to which legacies have been allocated in previous years will now soar!

Apart from playing with legacies, some charities present their revenues in two parts: 'general income' and 'benevolent income'. It may be difficult for the charity to decide what appears in what; it is even more difficult for the lay reader. The distinction appears to be drawn by some charities between money which is just sent in or raised for broad needs, the overall aims of the charity (called 'general income') and money sent in for a special purpose, say a named bed in a home (called 'benevolent' income). The idea can be appreciated to some extent but it does not make the task of interpreting the accounts any easier. One charity at least actually charges its fairly hefty auditing fee against the 'benevolent' review!

The ideal set of charity accounts would show unambiguously just what it cost to run each section of the organization and would distinguish between (1) the prime objects of the charity, the 'benevolent' aspect, (2) education of the public in the needs involved, for example by advertising, exhibitions, pamphlets and other publicity material, (3) administration costs and (4) fund-raising costs. The abiding difficulty is obviously in deciding what are administration expenses. The National Council of Social Service reported on this point:

> With further help from the accounting profession it might be possible to provide satisfactory guidance as to what should be involved in the accounts of charities under the heading of administration expenses, but we ourselves feel unable to suggest a definition which would be sufficiently clear or acceptable in the case of all charities. Our view is that administration expenses are those of central management and organization of the society's affairs, i.e. secretarial, accounting, etc., other activities at national headquarters being classed as services in connection with the prime objects of the society or as fund-raising. This definition however does not provide much practical guidance and there is a special problem for charities

with a small staff, where of necessity one individual carries out multifarious duties, being for example both welfare worker and administrator, and where much of the welfare work is also of an administrative nature.

The Charity Commissioners, it will be recalled, said the same thing. But, when all is said and done, it should not be impossible to break down some costs fairly clearly. If a man has a multiple role in a charity, his cost could be allocated, say, 50 per cent to administration, 25 per cent to fund-raising, and 25 per cent to specific welfare work. Cost accountants in the commercial world do this sort of thing all the time.

Note that the National Council report specifically recommended that accountancy be included in administrative expenses. Yet, as we have seen, some charities include under the 'charitable' or 'benevolent' accounts the cost of the annual audit and this can take quite a load off administrative costs as presented in the accounts because, whoever does well or poorly out of charity work, auditors in general do extremely well. Their fees are high and getting higher, and £1,500 for auditing the accounts of a not very large charity is quite usual. Some auditors, however, give their services free or very nearly so.

Fund-raising costs, as distinct from administrative, are not simple either and vary according to what method of raising money is used. There are, first of all, straightforward appeals in which the public is simply asked to give money. There are functions which provide a show of some kind, for example, on which the charity hopes to make a profit. And then there are multi-purpose appeals which may have broader objectives than the immediate accumulation of cash – for instance to form public opinion on the necessity of helping with a particular problem, to educate them to a new need, and to encourage of long-term giving such as covenants. We have noted that the costs of fund-raising rise when the economic climate is poor and the need is greatest.

The National Council working party minced no words in its approach to fund-raising costs, recommending bluntly: "All charities should endeavour to show the gross amount of their appeal proceeds together with the related expenditure thereon." The report provided a list of items of expenditure that might generally come under fund-raising costs. They are: (1) cost of materials for house-to-house and street collections, such as envelopes, emblems, trays, collecting tins, collector's badges and the like; (2) postage, printing and dispatch costs for postal appeals; (3) salaries and expenses of appeals organizers and supporting staff, together with allied overheads; (4) advertising, including display posters; (5) the cost of promotional material such as leaflets, films and magazines for regular subscribers; and (6) fees of fund-raising and public relations consultants, together with items such as the cost of administering the appeal staff where this is a separate function as opposed to the general administration of the charity, and including the cost of senior and managerial staff when engaged on fund-raising. It is suggested that displays and promotions which have no fund-raising connotation should be shown separately – for example educational material encouraging children to clean their teeth or urging people to avoid accidents in the homes. Where a local organization deducts expenditure before passing on the balance to headquarters, local accounts should be produced and made available not only locally but to the national body.

As a generalization, the report thought that where local costs had been deducted, large national charities might find their fund-raising costs working out at around 15 per cent of voluntary income, but smaller charities (those in advance of their time and perhaps socially unacceptable as yet to many people) and new charities will have widely varying expense ratios. They added: "If charities have a substantial and reasonably steady income from legacies this should be shown in a manner which will relate it to other appeals income, so that the whole of the proceeds will be seen in relation to the advertising and fund-raising costs of the organization."

In the section of its report dealing with charity accounting, the working party drew attention to the variety of aims and methods of charities and concluded that there was, at present, no common mould into which the accounts of all charities could be forced for presentation. Charities that are incorporated bodies, under Royal Charter, the Industrial and Provident Societies Acts, the Friendly Societies Acts or the Companies Acts, are already subject to a certain amount of statutory control over the form and content of their accounts and the responsibilities of their auditors, but unincorporated charities, of which there are many, large and small, are free from such control except through the limited powers of the Charity Commissioners. Suggesting the preparation of a guide to standards of accounting and financial reporting for charities, the working party said that under 'income', money from the following sources should be specified and distinguished in public accounts: (1) funds raised and accounted for to the parent or national organizations by autonomous branches or independent supporting groups; (2) substantial block grants, showing the source in each case – for example Government departments, charitable trusts and foundations, and so on; (3) legacies; (4) investments, bank deposits, etc; (5) trading activities – normally the net profit or net receipts, provided that detailed trading accounts supporting the figures are appended or are otherwise available on request by the public; (6) receipts for services provided, for example from Government or local authority sources; and (7) any other source of income significant by comparison with the total income.

The working party did not say so, but anyone who has studied enough charity accounts will know that some charities concerned in trading go to almost any lengths to conceal operating details; they take the attitude that this would only help competitors in their particular fields. And the losses incurred, often by sheer inefficiency, by some of the trading divisions of certain charities, are by no means small. Some such charities will say that as the trading keeps incapacitated people in happy employment, it does not matter if it makes a profit or not. The two aims are by no means incompatible as many other charities have shown.

Under the heading of 'expenditure' the working party recommended the following headings: (1) the prime functions for which the charity exists – grant aid, social work, medical research; (2) administration; (3) fund-raising; (4) general instruction of the public to create a climate of opinion conducive to the objects of the charity where this expenditure has no direct fund-raising connotations; (5) legacies – what is done with them should be clearly disclosed; and (6) gifts in kind.

Gifts in kind – yes. Some charities never mention them at all! But there is clearly a need for records where the value of gifts in kind is material, and the working party suggested that their estimated value should be clearly shown in monetary terms, with the basis of the valuation employed also explained. It is emphasized that any value put upon gifts in kind for accounts purposes should be related only to those gifts that have been sold for cash or passed on to beneficiaries of the charity.

Because auditors are not responsible for seeing that charities give all the details that the public, not to mention the Charity Commissioners, need, there have been suggestions for some sort of code of conduct for charity accountancy. But accountants are at least as conservative as charities: none of the bodies involved seems to want such a code or even think it desirable, and without legislation it would be impossible to enforce. That idea is definitely a dead duck.

So also appear to be proposals for a code of conduct for charity fund-raising generally. The charities take the view that even if it were possible to enforce such a code – which they doubt – it would give a bad impression of charity work to the media and to the public, implying that charities could not be trusted to run their own affairs individually. The arguments against any such code were perhaps summed up by the Royal National Institute for the Blind in a submission to the working party: "We feel that it would be highly damaging to the cause of charity to attempt to construct such a code and even more so to attempt to embark upon a scheme for publicizing it. The general image that the public has of charity is, we believe, that our administration may be well-meaning and woolly but that our standard of rectitude is high. Any publicity that suggests that we have failed in the latter respect would be infinitely more harmful than any minor transgression of an isolated nature."

The working party, however, felt that a fund-raising code could help genuine charities and improve efficiency. A code ensuring financial probity and one which checked that every charity operated within its charitable limits should have legal force and be supplemented by a voluntary code providing guide lines. The working party did not want a *Government* code, at any price, but said:

> We do not think it would be right for us to report that there was no need for a fund-raising code of any sort. We are satisfied that the existing legal and other sanctions are sufficient to deal with the very rare cases relating to dishonesty or failure to serve charitable purposes, and that the emphasis should be on guidance to charities to enable them to fulfil better their charitable functions rather than to restrain them. There are certain rules in relation to fund-raising which we consider should be of universal application. It is possibly more important that these should be supplemented by more general and discursive guidance on a variety of topics which affect the fund-raising efficiency of charities and that this should take the form, on the one hand of aiding charities and on the other of educating the public on the philosophy, attitude and problems of charities in connection with fund-raising and all that is involved in fund-raising by charity.

Any code that ever emerged would, one thinks, largely be concerned with the operations of 'fringe charities' rather than the ones whose objectives are well known. There are possibly three things needed above all in this area. The first is that any charity appeal should make crystal clear the objects for which money or help is required and whether the proceeds will be applied directly or through other agencies. The second is that if the operation involves the deduction of expenses before the balance of the proceeds is passed on to one or more charities, then this must be made clear, especially if the appeal is by commercial or non-charity interests or by trading concerns. The third is that promotors appealing on behalf of an existing charity, using its name, should secure the permission of the charity concerned and name it in the appeal, with the address; they should have to account to the charity involved for the proceeds of the appeal. Remember that by giving its authority for this kind of operation, the charity accepts responsibility for the appeal.

It is when one tries to question some charities about their financial activities, above all about presentation of their accounts, that a less pleasant side of charity administration comes to the fore. Some of the men, and women, running Britain's charities are openly arrogant in their reactions to inquiries from the public. One reason *may* be the high percentage of retired Service officers in the ranks of the administrators! Men who have been more or less forced into early retirement from the Army, Navy or Air Force are not automatically the best people to run a complex business, where the ability to command is of less importance than the ability to understand, or commercial wisdom. There are men running charities who are openly described by their staffs as combining authoritarianism and indolence. "They get away with it under the Old Boy network . . . which is how they secured their jobs in the first place", said a senior technician in one of the biggest organizations. "Some have lost the power of decision-taking – if they ever had it; others are too darn precipitous. Both types know that if they make a mistake, nobody is going to call them seriously to account."

There is no doubt about the integrity of these men or, indeed, their dedication to their particular causes; in most cases they are real fanatics here. But if you add to the small army of the retired, the retinue of ageing office females (some of them right 'battle-axes' in dealing with inquirers, nearly all of them overly protective of their bosses), one can see why even the charity industry itself admits at times to 'woolliness'. This ranges from sending out appeals twice or thrice to the same people, through failing to 'key' their advertising appeals so that they do not know which medium has secured the best results, to the much more expensive mistake of 'selling soft' on investments. Few of the type of people described here have much idea of stocks and shares or financial dealings generally and practically none of them even claim to understand, or at least care to expound on, their own organization's accounts if they are at all obscure. That is one reason why some charities show losses in their trading concerns. And the 'tea party committees' which back up the failed generals and admirals may be charming and gracious, but they are also in many cases monumentally ineffective!

Hence the emphasis on professionalism by everyone who takes an objective look at charity. Many of the truly efficient charities today will have nothing to do any more with voluntary or 'cheap' assistance. Charities rely greatly on whoever may be their central moving spirit, the director or general secretary. He in turn relies in one direction on his committee of management or executive committee and on the other on his technical and office staff. Dealing, for example, with thousands of envelopes containing cash or cheques calls for considerable efficiency – a girl must be able to recognize a faulty cheque incorrectly written out, and do it at speed.

"I'd rather have one day a week of the services of a professional, at any level, than six from an amateur," said the head of one of the largest charities in the country.

15

ORGANIZING THE EMOTIONS

A constant generalized charge against charity is that the various societies operate a mass conspiracy to organize the emotions, by fair means and foul, in order to extract the last penny for what often seem to be obscure aims, if not sometimes deliberate misrepresentations. Certainly, much criticism of charity advertising and appeals in the past was thoroughly justified, on a number of different counts, but now the major organizations have learned the lesson of the public backlash that undoubtedly developed in some cases and have become much more professional in their techniques. In any event, press advertising has – like much else – become too expensive for a lot of charities. Gone are the days when Oxfam's advertisement in the *Sunday Times* at a cost of £420 produced £19,600, or a return of £1 for every 2p spent. ITV does not accept advertisements from charities because it is generally agreed that to do so would give an unfair advantage to the really wealthy societies at the expense of the poorer and sometimes more deserving, ones.

A lot of the criticism of press advertising by charities has centred on the vagueness of the appeal, the absence of a specified, recognized objective. This is not invariably a valid criticism. The National Council of Social Service report, discussing wrong advertising approaches by charities, made the point that their advertising was often needed "to open men's hearts and minds to the need for charity not only in terms of money". Long-term goodwill and confidence may be more important to a charity than the immediate financial response. There is often – especially with some new charities, perhaps with modern social aims – a greater need to educate opinion on a broad front rather than to appeal directly for immediate cash.

The Charity Commissioners described the form and content of advertisements and appeals material as the most difficult and controversial of subjects. The Commissioners sent to the working party 87 criticisms of charity advertising, gathered over five years. Of these, ten complaints related to the high cost, of which three were from the Commissioners themselves and four were from the public. Of 19 expressions of doubt as to whether contributions were applied to the purposes for which they were given, 13 were from the public, two from other charities, and one from the Commissioners. Out of 59 complaints about the accuracy or technique of an appeal, 23 were from the public, four from Members of Parliament, six from other charities, 12 from the press, and nine from the Commissioners. Five charities complained about being forced to follow high-pressure advertising techniques. The working party report divided all the complaints into two categories.

> The first consists of complaints against what might be called hard-hitting advertisements, that is to say the use of emotive words and pictures and sensational matter and presentation which may be shocking and horrifying to some people. The second category amounts to complaints of misrepresentation, the use of insufficiently authenticated pictures, an ambiguous text, the giving of an incorrect impression as to the use of money, and the manipulation of type-sizes so that a true impression can only be obtained by reading the smaller print. These two different categories are lumped together as presenting various dangers: the danger that the image of charity will tarnished as charities demonstrate that any ends justify the means; that other charities will be forced to abandon their more conservative methods, resulting in what the former Chief Charity Commissioner described as 'debasement of the currency.' In anticipation of the answer that when it ceases to pay, charities will stop, it is said that by that time charity will have been permanently damaged.

In fact since that report was first published charities have largely changed their approach – they saw the red light. Said the working party:

> It is often difficult to decide where exaggeration produced by enthusiasm for a cause ends and where misrepresentation begins. It is clear to us that the word 'refugees' should not be used where all that is meant is foreigners away from their home country . . . We think that misrepresentation often results from the insider failing to appreciate how his appeal will look to the public. We had a complaint from a man who had given a donation at the door to 'Animal Rescue' on the strength of pamphlets which merely gave the initials B.U.A.V. instead of British Union for the Abolition of Vivisection. This is not in fact a charity but a letter to the society

produced a prompt reply from their general secretary saying that, in view of the complaint, when the leaflet was reprinted the full title of the society would appear. The Sailors' Children's Society frankly stated in their evidence to us that, although their activities covered children, seamen's welfare, aged seafarers and Merchant Navy hostels, their appeal to the public in recent years had been wholly on behalf of children. If people responded to the appeal for children but their money helped seamen, this constitutes misrepresentation. Unless it can be shown that all the money from the particular appeal has gone to children, the wording of the advertisement must not conceal the fact that adults are also helped.

The working party felt that the style of advertising, fund-raising and publicity material from many charities could be criticised only on the grounds that "it is too conservative, compromising, and unimaginative adequately to serve those in need of charitable aid". To justify costs, the standard of creativity must be high and can only be obtained with the help of professional advice. Urging the continued use of modern advertising techniques, the working party commented: "However brilliant and in some eyes questionable these techniques and skills may be, no charity will retain the active interest of its supporters unless it can continue to convince them that the problem remains unsolved and that its efforts to tackle it are sound and are producing good results."

Incidentally, the Trade Descriptions Act of 1968 does *not* cover false claims about charities if the appeal is solely to gather donations. The Act deals with false claims made in the course of trade or business and where the claims are applied to goods or relate to services provided. If the charity provides goods or services, then its claims are covered by the Act – for example if goods are falsely claimed to have been made by disabled persons.

A number of charities, notably those connected in one way or another with children, have not only cut down drastically on press advertising but eliminated those forlorn pictures of the past. The view is increasingly taken that if an advertisement *isolates* a child, puts it into some sort of ghetto, it does more harm than good. The problem for the advertising charity is to make people feel sorry for the victims while avoiding wallowing in sentiment. For example, the Royal National Institute for the Blind now concentrates on the good, the active things that the blind can do, not on the pathos of their situation. An advertisement showing a girl on a diving board, for example, reads 'Susie can do everything . . . but see'. The blind have a much more powerful appeal than the deaf. "A blind person appears pathetic while the deaf reveal nothing", said one fund-raiser. In the same way, Barnardo's have set their faces against heart-tugging appeals; they rightly hold that if a system used for raising money sets a child apart, it simply should not be used.

A famous example of the horrific was the Salvation Army advertisement with a photograph of an old soldier reduced more or less to a pile of bones and the headline 'For God's Sake Care, give us a pound'. It worked magnificently for a time. The advertising agencies say that television and the Press have made people almost blasé about pure tragedy. People shut their eyes determinedly to images of despair, death and vividly-presented disease and shun the particular charity thereafter. A different approach has to be found. The Salvation Army, conscious that certain styles of 'glossy' advertising can give a quite unwanted plush image to a charity, launched a new-style campaign towards the end of 1973, and very different it was from 'For God's Sake Care . . .'. Their posters showed a Salvation Army officer carrying and comforting a small, crying child. Nothing too horrific in that. Each poster carried a 'thank you' message to a leading company mogul . . . in the hope that other companies would give money and be named on future posters. Mild blackmail?

The Blue Cross animals' charity, to take another instance, does not show starving or trapped animals. Their advertisements seek to combine the practical and the sentimental: a picture of a dog, its owner, and a nurse, perhaps a kitten snuggling up to the dog. Once they tried an experiment with different animals. They raised a lot of money from a picture of a horse, very little from a cat, almost nothing from a dog. Perhaps because the dog was not seen as a guide for the blind?

The Save the Children Fund has also dropped its pictures of dying children, while the Cheshire Foundation virtually never uses any money for paid advertising. They have a budget of £100 a year for staid appeals for legacies in legal publications, usually around Christmas.

The public reaction to charity advertisements was analyzed by a market research organization, Everett's Marketing, which said:

Attempts to illustrate what is done with the money collected

> cannot be buried in the body copy, where they are simply not recognized as achievements but as extensions of the original appeal; that is, however, worded, they are read as 'we need *for* . . .' not as 'We used the money *to* . . .' The most favourable reaction to appeals through the media is elicited by those which state a target and indicate when this target is achieved . . . The television programme *Blue Peter* was acclaimed for the way in which it set about collecting for charities; the main points in its favour were (a) that it set specific targets and described explicitly what had been achieved with the donations so that there was a pleasant feeling of self-congratulation at the achievement among contributors and (b) that it collected objects for which respondents no longer had any use – old knives and forks and dinky cars for example. Collections of old newspapers by Scouts and milk bottle tops for guide dogs for the blind were also commended. Thus it seems clear that while the public are not hostile to the basic aims of charities, because they resent deeply being forced into a position where they cannot refuse to give money they become hostile to charities themselves. Admiration for a cause soon becomes animosity if money is involved unless there is either a direct personal relationship or a visible effect from the donation.

Public emotional reaction is nowhere better reflected than in the responses to radio and TV appeals. These are supervised by a joint BBC/ITV Appeals Advisory Committee. ITV broadcasts 12 appeals a year, the BBC many more on radio and TV. In the year to March 1973 BBC TV appeals raised £193,592 and Radio 4 raised a further £208,918. Appeals range in an average year from £200 to £300 from a regional broadcast on sound to tens of thousands from TV, especially for children's charities. An appeal on BBC 1 during the 1972/73 year for playgrounds for children's seaside holidays raised £38,858. The annual Radio 4 Christmas broadcast for the Wireless for the Blind Fund brought in £47,184.

However, the really big money rolls in for disasters. The BBC, ITV and the Press between them raised £340,000 for victims of the Nicaragua earthquake. No less than £1.48m was subscribed in 1970 in response to radio and TV appeals for victims of the East Pakistan cyclone and £1.2m for the India-Pakistan war sufferers. These major disaster appeals are now handled by the Disaster Emergency Committee, representing the British Red Cross, Christian Aid, Oxfam, War on Want and the Save the Children Fund. One function of the committee is, so far as possible, to ensure that the money subscribed does in fact go to the purposes for which a particular appeal was made.

The impact of children's needs was shown in what happened with Britain's own disaster, when 116 children and 28 others died in the coal tip avalanche at Aberfan in South Wales. The British public subscribed more to this than any other such charity appeal in this country, and raised £1.5m which, with interest, grew to £2m. To be truthful, the fund was grossly over-subscribed for the needs – which is what happens quite often. Before the Aberfan fund was wound up early in 1972, six years after the disaster, about £1.2m was paid out in grants to parents and others, £65,000 was spent on a cemetery memorial, £25,000 for a memorial garden, and £150,000 towards the removal of the local coal tips – something which it might be thought the National Coal Board should have paid for entirely. With the balance of the money a community centre costing no less than £350,000 was built. Understandably there was a great deal of criticism of some of the ways in which the money was expended, but it had, of course, to be spent in ways approved by the Charity Commissioners, who, dealing in one of their annual reports, with disaster funds generally, commented: "One of the fundamental rules of law relating to property given for specific charitable purposes is that such property shall not be diverted to other purposes except under proper authority and then only if the original purpose has been fulfilled or is no longer capable of achievement either wholly or in part. Neither we nor the court have power to ignore this rule . . ."

Referring to the £1.46m raised for the East Pakistan Cyclone Fund, the Commissioners noted that the wording of the appeal referred both to immediate aid for victims and for their rehabilitation. Under the direction of the Disasters Emergency Committee the five charities it comprises combined their efforts to provide immediate relief in the form of medical aid, food, blankets and clothing. Then each charity used its share of the remaining money to pursue its own policies for rehabilitation and housing. But this was interrupted by the war in Bangladesh and the charities had to suspend activities. Suggestions were made that the unspent money be used for relief of the refugees from East Pakistan fleeing to India, but the Charity Commissioners ruled that, while there was no legal objection to the charities using the available funds for the relief of refugees from the area devastated by the cyclone, any attempt to discriminate between refugees from the cyclone and those from war-torn areas would obviously be extremely difficult. In the event, the Disasters Emergency Committee launched a new appeal specifically for the war sufferers. The Commissioners commented:

> It is easy to appreciate how, when there is an emergency such as that created by the flood of Pakistani refugees into India, a strong feeling may arise that a sum of money recently collected for use in the same general area should be diverted to meet the pressing new need. But it is important to preserve the principle that money given for a particular charitable purpose shall not be put to any other use so long as the purpose to which it was given can still be achieved, and it is perhaps worth recording that even in the present case we received some objections to the suggestion that any of the money collected for the East Pakistan Cyclone Fund should be used for the relief of refugees in India.

The Commissioners pointed out that anyone drawing up an appeal for money because of a particular disaster or situation should bear in mind the desirability of including in the terms of the appeal suitable wording which, if more money became available than was required to meet the immediate need, would enable any surplus to be used for some related purpose.

As a further example of the difficulties that can arise here, the Commissioners recalled the appeal by the Royal Society for the Prevention of Cruelty to Animals for money to rescue sea birds affected by oil from the sinking of the tanker *Torrey Canyon* in 1967. About £33,000 was subscribed but only £10,000 could be spent at the time. The Society wanted to use the balance of the money for the general rescue and treatment of birds contaminated by oil pollution but since the original appeal made no reference to any purpose other than the *Torrey Canyon* victims, it was necessary for the Charity Commissioners to make a cy-près scheme some years later to permit broader use of the money.

The British, then, give generously to children, animals, medicine and foreign disasters – after Aberfan there has been marked reservation in reactions to tragic domestic events. What, by and large, they do not give at all generously to are the 'unpopular' charities – many of them among the most deserving and hard-working and in the greatest need just because so few people support them. In this bracket come charities for ex-prisoners and for law reform, those to help prostitutes, homosexuals – above all – and drug addicts. Even certain charities appealing for money for the homeless have difficulty because 'homeless' are now widely associated to the public mind with 'hippies', squatters and the like and there are strong political undertones in this area. The unpopular causes are just not emotive . . . one reason being that people cannot, or will not, identify themselves with the plight of the ex-prisoner, or any 'sinner'. Organization of emotion can only go so far.

16

THE 'MOST EFFICIENT'

Charities are jealous organizations by nature and quite a proportion of their spokesmen and women can rarely be induced to say a good word about a rival fund-raising society: they are far more likely to offer a criticism such as "*They're* too autocratic . . ." or "A pompous crowd that!" There is one great exception. Every single charity official asked by the author which organization was the best-run replied "Barnardo's". The unaminous verdict was: "The most efficient of them all".

Dr Barnardo's is also far and away the best-known charity among the public and leads all others in the general esteem in which it is held although not many people fully appreciate the wide range of work undertaken by this immense organization with a staff in the United Kingdom alone of 2,400 and a yearly expenditure, *directly on charitable work*, of around £4m. pounds. Strangely, in the light of other criticisms and queries about charities, very few of the public question the need for Barnardo's work, and to those who do bring up that old point that the State should undertake it all, Barnardo's will reply that the State has not got enough money, or at least not enough allocated to the Social Services. Many of the children in Barnardo's care are passed on to them by local authorities who have no room for them in State homes.

Barnardo's take in or help in some way every child they can within the scope of their finances and today they have about 6,000 under their wing in the United Kingdom, including Northern Ireland, of which about 3,000 are in residential care (in a Barnardo home) or with foster parents. This figure is lower than in past years because a tremendous change is coming over Barnardo's, with less emphasis being placed on looking after children actually in the society's homes and more in preventing the need for them ever arriving there. Social changes in Britain are dictating Barnardo's policy to a great extent. With the more affluent society, there is less need in certain areas of the country for residential care and Barnardo's have been closing down homes in relatively well-off counties, such as Kent, where local authorities can afford to do more, but expanding their work in the Midlands and similar areas of need. Today, too, no less than 25 per cent of all children under Barnardo's care are coloured and the pressures of the immigrant population are still increasing. Considering that the number of coloured people in the United Kingdom was estimated at the beginning of 1974 to be about 1.5m men, women and children, or very roughly two per cent of the entire population, the coloured child proportion under care is extremely high.

Ever since 1968 Barnardo's has been changing its 'image' and getting away from the archetypal Victorian look it wore for decades. Management consultants were brought in to strengthen the organization and today they operate from a glamorous five-storey steel and concrete headquarters at Ilford, Essex, set among the cottages that form 'The Village', the largest of the society's 100 residential units in the United Kingdom. Apart from the residential units and hostels, Barnardo's have a large foster parents organization, special schools for physically and mentally handicapped children, and for the educationally sub-normal, 'community homes' for children who have appeared before the courts, a family rehabilitation scheme, and of course their general preventative work and after-care for Barnardo's Old Boys and Old Girls. They have also homes in Australia and New Zealand.

That is just a brief summary of the unique organization that grew from the work of Thomas John Barnardo, born on 4 July 1845, at Upper Gardiner Street, Dublin. In April 1866 he arrived to train as a doctor at the London Hospital in Whitechapel with a view to becoming a missionary in China. London at that time was a city of overwhelming contrast – enormous and ostentatious wealth side by side with appalling poverty and in some areas, an almost total lack of sanitation and hygiene. An epidemic of Asian cholera swept the city, killing 8,000 people, and Thomas Barnardo was brought daily, hourly, face to face with all the tragedy and suffering as, with other medical students called in to help, he went on his rounds in the East End of London, doing whatever could be done. He saw literally hundreds of youngsters, half-naked and starving, sleeping huddled together wherever they could find a place, under tarpaulins in the markets, behind street hoardings, in barrels and baskets – anywhere the police could not see them. For the penalty of being found was prison! By

October Barnardo had made the first move in this hitherto uncaring world. With a few friends he opened a 'ragged school' in a disused donkey stable in Hope Place, Stepney. One evening one of the boys, named Jim Jarvis, stayed behind, pleading to be allowed to spend the night by the fire. Barnardo gently told him that he must go home. Jim replied simply that he had no home and Barnardo was horrified – even he had as yet no real idea how bad conditions were. Jim later took Barnardo around to show him the totally homeless like himself, who were penniless, roaming the streets, living on scraps, dressed in rags. There were also children who begged or stole or worked for a few pennies that enabled them to buy a bed in a common lodging house.

Now a man named Mick Farrell took Barnardo, dressed as a tramp, dirty and unshaven, to some of these lodging houses where, seeing and smelling the conditions, the young doctor decided there was plenty of work for him in Britain. For three years he campaigned, striding round the East End by day, preaching and selling bibles, and by night hunting out unwanted and destitute children to whom he could give food and shelter. A Mr Samuel Smith, M.P. one of the many who came to be impressed by Barnardo's sheer bravery and persistence, gave him £1,000 to open his first home, at Stepney Causeway, in September 1870.

This home had to be limited to boys only, though there were at least as many girls in need. The reason was that in those days it would have been considered 'improper' for a charity for girls to be administered by a bachelor! In 1873, however, Thomas Barnardo married Syrie Elmslie and as a wedding present was given a property at Ilford, to be used for the benefit of girls. This became 'The Village'. Years later the situation was brought before the Charity Commissioners when the society asked them to lift another Victorian taboo and permit the trustees to admit boys as well as girls to 'The Village'. Agreeing to do so, the Commissioners recorded in their annual report for 1971: " . . . By 1970 the whole trend of thought on management of homes for children had moved away from the institutional idea. It had come to be regarded as vastly preferable to house the children in groups of small homes and in order to achieve the feeling that they were part of a family, it was essential to have boys and girls, and particularly brothers and sisters, together. In support of this view the trustees had said that the Home Office would no longer make grants except to mixed homes. The homes still run by Dr Barnardo's entirely for girls were for those with special needs, such as the mentally handicapped."

When Dr Barnardo died in 1905, no less than 60,000 children had been helped and many homes established. Today the figure is almost a quarter of a million.

From the start, Dr Barnardo always tried to find work for the boys and girls on leaving his homes but this was often not possible in those hard times. Moreover, many of the children had been taken from criminal or plain bad parents, who often sought to take them away from the homes by force. Thus began the process of sending older children to the growing lands of the Empire, Canada in particular. The first party of specially selected Barnardo boys went to Canada in 1882 and many more mixed parties followed. At first the reception was hostile: the Canadians' view was that their country was merely being used as a dumping ground for waifs and strays and they did not want children with criminal backgrounds. Barnardo went to Canada personally and arranged to send out only boys and girls of good health and good character and with a grounding in a trade. At the time of his death he had sent 17,000 children to Canada. Since 1921 smaller numbers of children have emigrated to Australia, where there are now ten Barnardo homes which take in the young emigrants and help with Australian child-care problems generally. The first party of 47 Barnardo boys to arrive in Australia, on 24 October 1921, were the sons of British ex-Servicemen who had fallen in World War I. Fifty years later the first Barnardo's home was opened in New Zealand as a day-care and unmarried mothers' unit.

Increasingly today Barnardo's put their Family Care Service first. This is where it all begins. The underlying theme of the service is that the child should be seen not as an isolated unit but in relation to parents and relatives, who may need help also. The idea is to help families in difficulties, and deserted, widowed, separated and single mothers to remain responsible for their children. Small money grants are made, so long as the mother is already drawing every State allowance possible; there are regular visits from Barnardo social workers, and practical help ranges from providing a bicycle for a fatherless child to supplying furniture, clothing, shoes, even a TV set to relieve the boredom of the deserted wife. Home helps can be provided for desperately tired or ailing mothers or housekeepers for fathers trying to look after children without a wife.

The Family Care Service may have to work for months, even years, to help single parents and their families. Apart from practical problems such as money, there are almost always emotional difficulties of some kind among the children – truancy, nightmares and later perhaps theft and vandalism. Then there is the stress on the wives, the times when the pressures of life become too great to bear alone. The deserted or widowed wife and the single-handed father, worry equally where they can leave their children while they go out to work. The mother living at the top of a tower block is often penned in by her children isolated from any place in which to play. Others have large families crowded into one or two rooms. Hence the increasing drive to set up day-care centres, which are open from eight a.m. to six p.m. Here the children can be parked safely while mother works or even rests for a few hours. At these centres a small charge is made. Always the aim of the service is to do whatever will help to keep the family together.

However, this often proves impossible or unwise. Then if a child cannot be helped by the local authority, it is admitted to a Barnardo's home, in line with the Doctor's famous sign 'No destitute child ever refused admission', from which the homes became known as the 'Ever Open Door'. The children are, when possible, taken into homes closest to their parents or relatives and every effort is made to see that the parents keep in touch with them – some people cope with their own guilt feelings by shrugging off all responsibility once the home has taken over. The children go out to school like others, share in neighbourhood activities, and come back to a home life like that of any normal family, a far cry from the Victorian institution. The homes may hold from a dozen children up to 40 or so and the children's ages range from a few months up to 17 or 18 years. Whatever the size of the home, the children live as a family in small groups, each in its own part of the house and with its own house parents or, in the case of the latest homes, in separate flats or cottages. The children get ordinary pocket money too. For a four-year old it is currently about 7p, rising to about £1 at the age of 17.

For the very youngest with no forseeable prospect of returning to his own home or for the older child needing the intimacy of a small family, a good foster home is often the best solution. Barnardo's have more than a thousand children in such homes, which are visited regularly by the society's own social workers. Here Barnardo's pays for maintenance and clothing, and again provides pocket money, as it does for children living in lodgings or hostels.

In the same way that no child is refused admittance, none

is ever forced out of a Barnardo home before he or she is ready. Barnardo's profoundly believe that, before they leave the society's care, the children should be self-reliant and self-disciplined and they point to the fact that the school-leaving age is an even more critical time for boys and girls who have grown up in Barnardo's homes because they are facing not only leaving school and starting work, but also leaving perhaps the only home they have ever known. When possible, the older boys and girls get their own sitting rooms. All are taught basic home management and how to care for their clothes and manage their money. There is career guidance of course and then when the youngsters do leave and go out to work they are visited regularly by a social worker until they are 18, and longer if necessary. Barnardo's also runs a number of small hostels for boys and girls who are working but not yet sufficiently independent to live in their own lodgings.

Hundreds of Barnardo children have, however, special problems. One in 500 children in Britain is born with a physical defect and Barnardo's have five residential schools for the physically handicapped, where physiotherapy and speech-therapy are integrated with the school curriculum and out-of-school activities range from swimming, canoeing and camping to 'pop' groups, dramatic societies and photographic clubs. 'The Princess Margaret School' at Taunton, Somersetshire, which was opened in 1966, was the first Barnardo's custom-built school for physically handicapped children. Princess Margaret is president of the society. Barnardo's have a special school for children with diabetic problems and here parents may also stay for a short time to learn how to deal with their children's condition. Another pioneering project is a long-stay nursery unit for babies suffering from multiple handicaps – physical, mental and social. Here, babies who would otherwise know no other life than a hospital ward are encouraged to develop in a warm and loving environment with skilled medical care and teaching facilities.

Children who are educationally sub-normal or emotionally disturbed are catered for at a number of special homes and schools – it is estimated that one in every ten children in Britain today is in need of special education. At Kilmarnock the society co-operated with the Scottish Education Authority – which provided 60 per cent of the cost – to build a school for senior maladjusted boys and girls in the 11-16 age group, all young people who find it difficult to cope with the strains and stresses of everyday life, including attending ordinary schools. One of the aims of the school is to find the area of work in which each child can achieve a certain amount of success and build on this so that on leaving he or she may go on either to further education or to work. At other schools Barnardo's have had remarkable successes with children previously classed as 'uneducatable'.

To do all this costs money . . . millions. And Barnardo's really knows how to obtain the funds. The society has something like 2,000 voluntary committees in the United Kingdom, mostly consisting of a dozen or so people, who raise money in every possible way: garden fêtes, dances, sponsored walks, even sponsored mountain climbs. One of the most novel fund-raising ideas, dreamed up by a Barnardo's Helpers group, was a 'hush-in'. The first occured at Branston near Lincoln, where 100 youngsters sat in a hall and spoke not a word for four hours; they raised £116.04. The idea was soon copied by other groups. Barnardo's does not get much money from Big Business or companies generally, but it does raise substantial sums through its National Farthing League whereby people, working mostly in factories, give a small sum, generally 2p, out of their weekly earnings. The name of the League stems from the day when a farthing was the standard donation and worth collecting. One result of business 'progress' – the greater use of computers and centralization of company accounts in, say, London or Glasgow – has meant that Barnardo's helpers have had to persuade managements to incorporate an extra instruction in the computers to take account of the weekly 2p deduction!

Barnardo's has an army of house-to-house collectors but, to avoid overlapping and to stem a decline which became perceptible in this source of revenue four years or so ago, the society concentrates all its house collecting into two weeks in March. There was also for a time a decline in flag day revenue, but a hard drive cured that. The society has a share in the Children's Day street collection in the London area and runs its own flag days outside the capital.

The advertising image has changed, getting away from the aura of poverty and distress, the Victorian technique, and concentrating more on happy 'Thank You' themes. There is also a certain amount of reminder advertising in legal journals, seeking legacies, which are immensely important to Barnardo's, averaging as they do more than *£2m a year*. The record single legacy received was £220,000 net from Canada but they are generally around £100, though £5 to £10 is not uncommon. There are thousands of former Barnardo boys and girls living round the world and many have become rich and famous. It is probably fair to say that most of those who could afford it have remembered Barnardo's in their wills. For example, the society's school for maladjusted boys at Southborough in Kent is named after Captain Meadows, an old Barnardo boy who became a sea captain and left his entire estate to the society in thanks for 'bringing me up', thus enabling this school to be built in 1938.

Barnardo's also trade, substantially. They began with Christmas cards and now issue a catalogue with a whole range of products costing from 15p or so to £20. Barnardo's Helpers members sell from this like any other mail order catalogue and it is also distributed in youth clubs, schools and social organizations which may retain a small percentage to help their own funds. Otherwise no Barnardo collector of any kind gets any commission whatever. Trading brings in about £20,000 net a year and has the added advantage of helping to advertise the society and raising something like another £20,000 a year in donations.

To keep in line with the other charities discussed in this book, the Barnardo's accounts for the year ended 31 March 1971 are taken here. Broadly, £2.8m was raised in ordinary income, including £1.5m in legacies and almost a quarter of a million from the National Farthing League. Nearly £950,000 came from receipts for maintenance paid by local authorities, relatives of children, and overseas branches. Expenditure on homes, schools and hostels, non-residential and overseas work was £3.4m. Fund-raising and information services cost just under £570,000, and administration £180,749. A number of unusual costs, including the expense of decimalizing the society's computer, and granting £225,000 to a new national Children's Centre to study the general welfare of children, left a deficit for the year of £272,180.

By 1973 Barnardo's ordinary reserves totalled £11.2m with endowment and trust funds realizing a further £2.8m. That £11.2m, however, will look very different by 1977. For as part of its adaptations to the new needs and to meet the appeals of local authorities for yet more help, the society is spending as much as £6.5m on capital projects, homes and schools in the new areas of need, while re-organization of the social work programme is costing about £1m. And, like the other charities, Barnardo's says wryly, "Because of inflation we are running hard to stand still."

Efficient in this as in other matters, Barnardo's sets out all divisions of expenditure clearly: its accounts are impeccable.

Out of every one pound raised by Britain's richest charity – apart from the Joint Palestine Appeal, which is not really comparable – 80½p is spent today on work among children in the United Kingdom. The figure of 12½p spend on fund-raising and educational work is particularly interesting. For it is a good example of the necessity for a charity of this type to form public opinion and promote interest in child-care, especially in the extension of preventive work. That 12½p includes not only the cost of collecting boxes, emblems, printing and postage, but also the salaries, pensions and expenses of people like appeal representatives and school and university lecturers who undertake this highly essential educational work. It is, then, remarkably low compared with many less complex charities and those with a much smaller need for informative work. With the size of the staff and the millions being administered, a figure of only 3p out of every one pound for head office administration is also low. Work among children abroad cost another 3p and 1p is spent on advertising.

17

LEARNING TO BE BLIND

Every year in England and Wales alone about 2,000 people between the ages of 16 and 65 are registered for the first time as blind persons. This figure excludes those born blind or outside the ages mentioned and there are probably today about 116,000 blind in the whole United Kingdom, of which more than 70 per cent will be over the age of 65. A relatively small number of people are blinded in accidents of various kinds; the majority lose their sight through some form of eye disease. Advances in medical science have meant that more people live longer – some to grow blind – and more children survive to adulthood. So blindness is unfortunately on the increase.

As with some other fields we have seen, there is a great deal of ignorance and some prejudice concerning blind charities, the most-often expressed criticism being that (a) there are too many collecting organizations and (b) that the war-blinded charity, St Dunstan's, must be 'redundant' today and should be merged – with its seemingly immense wealth – with the major blind charity, the Royal National Institute for the Blind. In fact the various collecting organizations for the blind are centralized to a considerable degree and overlapping is very much more apparent than real.

The R.N.I.B. will, if there is a successful local collecting organization in a given area, stay out of the way and receive a proportion of the collection. The R.N.I.B. does not collect in London for example, leaving it to the Greater London Fund for the Blind, and it has scores of similar arrangements throughout the United Kingdom. In the same way the Greater London Fund for the Blind has a number of smaller participating organizations of its own, simply because it has proved to be the most efficient form of collecting – people like to give locally. If, however, R.N.I.B. has reason to feel that a local organization is weak, it will organize collections itself and return a percentage to the particular local cause.

In its 1970/71 financial year the R.N.I.B. had an aggregate

gross income of £3,124,000. They spent £585,000 on nursery homes and schools, £235,000 on residential and holiday homes, £488,000 on rehabilitation, training and provision of employment, £943,000 on Braille facilities and their Talking Book library service, and sent £276,000 to other societies for the blind under the collecting system described. Less than 2p out of every one pound of the Institute's net income goes on central administration. Out of every one pound, the Braille work takes 21p. There are more than a quarter of a million Braille magazines and periodicals and 100,000 bound books distributed each year, as well as more than 500 different kinds of special aids for blind people, including a rain warning device that tells a blind housewife when her washing is getting wet! The Institute has centres for the rehabilitation and training of the newly blind, residential and holiday homes for both the blind and the deaf-blind, holiday hotels, a centre for blind adolescents, colleges for boys and girls either blind or with seriously defective sight, schools for blind children with additional handicaps, and a school for training blind physiotherapists. There is a special unit for training and helping the parents of blind children and a school for men and women who wish to train the blind to move about safely. The National Mobility Centre, as it is called, is run by a consortium of the R.N.I.B., St Dunstan's and the Birmingham Royal Institution for the Blind. Then there are the Sunshine Homes: residential nurseries for young blind children.

Training and rehabilitation and employment schemes take 20p from every one pound while the homes, schools, colleges and nurseries require 30p. The Talking Book Service – also run in conjunction with St Dunstan's – has a membership of about 37,000 and the Institute handles more than a million cassette recordings every year. In addition to general books of all kinds, there is a special service for students. The playing machines are supplied by the Institute at a nominal charge, which in many cases is paid by the local authority, and the provision of recordings is free. In addition, a national network of volunteers – electronics engineers, radio amateurs and the like – go out in their own time to service Talking Book machines in the blind people's own homes. In the vast majority of cases the authors of the books give permission for their work to be recorded for a nominal once-for-all payment of one pound. Talking books cost 16p per pound of income, while capital expenditure and other payments – new schools and centres constantly being opened, maintenance of existing establishments and so on – need a further 11p. Total – 98p out of every 100.

To run all this and pay for its staff of teachers, trainers, technicians, nurses, wardens, printers, secretaries and others, who total about 1,250 throughout the United Kingdom, and to organize the British Wireless for the Blind Fund, the Institute raises money from flag days, bazaars and the like, and collections (all collectors are salaried staff and nobody gets commission) but it concentrates its fund-raising efforts on securing legacies, covenants and donations, in that order. They have 16 kiosks, 14 of them in London, mostly installed in the offices of big companies and generally staffed by registered blind people, who are so adept at selecting packets of cigarettes or tobacco or bars of chocolate and handing over change that the customers often never realize they are blind at all.

R.N.I.B. has one shop only, at headquarters in London, where goods made by the blind are sold. In 1970/71 the Institute's trading activities brought in £319,377, but they cost £327,704 to operate. Their main purpose is to promote the better education, training, employment and welfare of the blind, not to garner revenue for the Institute. All the non-fund-raising activities of the year, such as schools, Braille publications and so on, brought in £1,265,656 but cost £2,091,742 to run. The balance had to be made up from appeals, gifts, donations and legacies. Appeals secured £702,357, and a further £63,000-plus came from the other collecting agencies under the centralized arrangement. The R.N.I.B., however, paid out much more to other societies, as we have seen. Legacies brought in £911,270. A total of £1,024,262 was transferred to the general charity funds and £80,675 put in special funds at the requests of donors. Investments and other income raised £141,000.

The Institute is very research-minded and its own technical department works on many projects from a simple telephone number memorizer to a specialized data-processing terminal – anything that will lesson the problems of the blind. They adapt or devise highly accurate scientific apparatus and have produced the world's smallest and most compact crossword puzzle for the blind.

With the increasing numbers of blind people in employment, there is a greater demand for Braille material of all kinds. During the 1970/71 year alone no less than 1,634 Braille volumes were added to the R.N.I.B. stock, most of them having been transcribed by volunteers working in their own homes and tackling some of the most difficult scientific, mathematical and linguistic material. A headquarters staff transcribes examination papers into Braille right up to university degree level. Braille is supplied for the training of computer programmers and telephone lists for switchboard operators, while the music department provides classical, standard and 'pop' Braille sheet music as well as material for music teachers and students. Refresher courses are held for blind music teachers. The Institute publishes Braille newspapers summarizing the important news, and when metrication was coming along it produced a guide to decimal money with a Braille version of the shoppers' conversion table. They make maps and globes for the blind and provide weekly summaries of football and cricket results – many deaf-blind people are pools addicts.

All in all it is an extraordinary range of activities. In the financial year 1971/72 the R.N.I.B.'s services to the blind cost £3,141,000, or £326,000 more than the previous year, representing the highest-ever annual expenditure of £27 for each registered blind person in Great Britain and Northern Ireland.

Even if only with its joint work with the R.N.I.B., it can be seen that the belief that St Dunstan's caters only for an almost vanished number of war-blinded is clearly not true, and the amount of assistance that St Dunstan's gives in the wider field of the blind is increasing each year. As the result of a bequest of money for people blinded 'whether on war service or otherwise', people under the age of 50 whose loss of sight is not connected with military service can be admitted to St Dunstan's for training, settlement in employment, and technical after-care.

St Dunstan's was founded in 1915 by Sir Arthur Pearson, himself blind and President of what was then the National Institute for the Blind, now the 'Royal National'. He established it for the training and after-care of all war-blinded men, and later women. The number of men and women blinded in war or warlike operations who have passed through St Dunstan's since 1915 is about 6,500, of whom 1,909 were alive in 1971. They included 633 who lost their sight as the result of service in World War I, and 1,276 from World War II and later disaster areas such as Korea, Malaya, Cyprus and – today – Northern Ireland.

During 1970/71 the total of new admissions was 41, of whom 23 were from World War I and 18 from World War II or later. Currently beneficiaries range in age from 90 to 25 and it can be actuarially shown that, assuming there are no more wars in which Britain is engaged, St Dunstan's will still have an active role to play under its original concept well into the 21st century.

Nonetheless St Dunstan's has, since the beginning of 1959 or so, progressively dismantled organized collections and they have not appealed for money at all for the past seven years, although they do rely on spontaneous donations and more particularly on legacies. The trouble is inflation. It has been calculated that at the present rate of inflation the £1 that was worth 20 shillings (or 100p) in 1938 will be worth only about 7p at the end of the century – and *that* calculation was made before the economic events of 1973 and 1974! Inflation eats up reserves as surely as ordinary expenditure and St Dunstan's believe that if they were not still receiving a certain amount of new money they might have to start appealing once more, and may yet have to do so unless inflation is contained.

It is important to bear in mind that while the after-care or social welfare of disabled people generally is now the responsibility of the local authorities, *in the case of blind ex-Servicemen and women this remains in practice exclusively the responsibility of St Dunstan's*, who consider that if they had to merge with any other organization, such as the R.N.I.B., there would be a great deterioration of the standard of care to which St Dunstaners have been accustomed, running directly counter to the wishes of the hundreds of thousands who have supported the organization financially since 1915.

At 31 March 1971 St Dunstan's had total assets of £16,573,175, of which about £2.5m was the value of properties such as homes, staff houses, headquarters, stores and so on. In the year 1970/71 donations and subscriptions came to only £15,445, but legacy revenue reached £945,650 and interest on investments to no less than £743,767. Against an aggregate gross income for the year of £1,704,862, expenditure on all purposes was £1,252,373, of which £1,174,425 went directly on relief work of one kind and another. Administrative and overhead expenses came to £150,948, or a little more than eight per cent.

Apart from its own work, over the past eleven years St Dunstan's has paid out £249,934 in grants to other organizations, £341,403 to the Talking Book Service, and £153,211 for experimental and research work on sensory aids for the blind.

All newly blinded men and women who come within St Dunstan's aegis go first to the magnificent residential training centre at Ovingdean, near Brighton, Sussex, which is also a holiday home. Here they will, in St Dunstan's phrase, 'learn to be blind' and equip themselves to enjoy as full a life in the world as possible. Preliminary training may take six months or more. Every trainee learns to type and some learn shorthand – a blind person can take down 120 words a minute on a Braille shorthand machine. On going out into the world, each St Dunstaner who can operate one is loaned a typewriter for life for use in his or her own home. As part of the preliminary work, trainees do woodwork and model-making and become familiar with Braille playing cards and dominoes. Many learn rifle-shooting and engage in most forms of outdoor sport. All this is aimed at developing their sense of self-confidence and the art of 'seeing' through the senses of touch and hearing.

Throughout the initial period the staff study each individual's ability, character and ambition so that when the time comes he or she can be helped to decide on a career. For some it is best for them to be able to work in their own homes and St Dunstan's supplies workshops that may be erected in their gardens if necessary. Home-workers receive raw materials at cost price or less and engage in an extensive variety of handicrafts, from mat and basket-making to boot-repairing. With the exception of the boots, all finished work which cannot be sold locally goes to St Dunstan's to be sold either wholesale to shops and large customers like British Rail and public authorities, or retailed through exhibitions, agricultural shows and various sales schemes. About a quarter of a million articles are sold in this way in an average year.

But for those who are suitable, much more advanced work, in a wider sphere, is preferable. At Ovingdean there is a machine shop where men can familiarize themselves with the factory background and learn to operate various machines. Today hundreds of war-blinded men are working in industry throughout the country, operating lathes and drills and all types of semi-automatic machines. Their work is not only comparable with their sighted workmates, in some cases output is greater. Apart from factory work, the blind are trained at Ovingdean in such occupations as physiotherapy – where blindness is actually an asset as the sense of touch is so remarkably developed – and telephone switchboard operating. Many employers say that the blind make the best operators here because they hear better, memorize better, and show more patience and tact. Numbers have been trained to run small retail shops, others poultry farms. Blind men and women have gone on to become doctors, parsons, solicitors, secretaries, actors, journalists, salesmen, schoolmasters, lecturers, chartered accountants and missionaries.

Once a man or a woman is trained and a suitable job found, St Dunstan's helps in the next and often vitally important stage, housing. A lot of St Dunstaners take up work in places where they have had no roots, and homes have to be found for them and for wives and families. The estate department will, if necessary, buy a suitable property and instal the St Dunstaner as tenant at a very reasonable rent. The property will be maintained free.

After-care covers a wide field. St Dunstan's has holiday and convalescent homes, one of which is also a permanent home for the aged and infirm who have nowhere else to go. Financial aid is provided, of course, money loaned to start businesses, and there is even a special scheme whereby St Dunstaners can insure their lives to protect their widows if the man dies first, which is more often the case than not. St Dunstan's pays half the premiums on such policies.

Numbers of the blind have other disabilities. Men and women have lost both arms as well as both eyes and St Dunstan's has a special research and experimental centre to develop every possible mechanical and scientific aid. Among the devices that have come from here are adaptations to radio sets (which enable the blind to switch on and tune in themselves), telephones, typewriters for people with artificial hands, watches which tell the time when a plunger is depressed, specially adapted kettles, and a cigarette machine which produces the cigarette already lighted. There are special electric razors, pipe-holding devices, an adaptor for vacuum cleaners, a change-giving machine, and another to enable blind shopkeepers to tell through a series of buzzer alarms what coin has been given to them. Musical instruments have been altered for the use of the handless – the most successful being trombones, vibraphones, xylophones and pianolas.

St Dunstan's proudly claims that over the past 60 years it has provided a more complete rehabilitation, training, settlement in employment, and after-care service for a special group of seriously disabled people than has any other organization anywhere in the world.

18

THE GREATEST CHALLENGE

Charities concerned with cancer have a relatively easy task in raising money, especially during the last few years when the whole subject has been brought out so much more into the open, yet, paradoxically, it is extremely difficult for them to show concrete results. It should be made clear at the start that these cancer charities can never in the foreseeable future have enough money or working manpower. There is no truth in the assertion that cancer charities have so much money that they do not know what to do with it.

The very word *cancer*, so evocatively named from the Latin for 'crab', frightens people and has done so through the ages, but there is a change in attitude today. Once famous people died 'after a long illness', their obituaries never recorded the fact that cancer was the cause, and it was only whispered by friends if they happened to find out. Most people were quite unaware of the extent, real and potential, of the dreaded disease. Perhaps Richard Dimbleby performed the greatest of his many services to the public when he ensured that the cause of his death should be widely known. Jack Hawkins also permitted the cause of his illness to be publicized. These men lifted a veil of the kind that had for generations hung over tuberculosis, another disease that was regarded almost as anti-social, certainly something of which to be ashamed and to be concealed so far as possible. Their example was quickly and increasingly followed while the general anti-smoking campaign cast a ruthless and continuing spotlight on the whole issue. Cancer was brought fully into the light of day.

Cancer appears to be as old as the animal world. One of the earliest examples, thought to be 350 million years old, is a fossilized fish with cancer of the jawbone. A treatise on human cancer survives on a papyrus of about 3,000 B.C. It was not, however, until the nineteenth century that much was known about the disease. Once it had been established that all living matter is composed of minute cells and that a normal growth of tissues on the repair of injuries is effected by a controlled multiplication of these cells through a process of division, there followed the recognition that cancer is essentially an *uncontrolled* multiplication of certain cells in the body without regard to the needs of the body as a whole. With some 200 different types of cancer, it remains the greatest challenge to medical science and an awe-inspiring one. It has been said that compared with the task facing cancer research workers, travel to the moon was a simple problem. Professor L.G. Lajtha, writing in the golden jubilee year report of the Cancer Research Campaign, said: "We know that the fundamental information, the 'blueprint', that regulates the behaviour of cells is 'printed' in a certain type of material in the cell – DNA. This 'message' is so complicated that if its code were to be represented in written words, the basic information in any *one* of our cells – and there are 3,000 times as many cells in a human body than there are people living on earth – would constitute a typewritten text of some 600,000 pages, a pile of papers over 50 yards high!"

However, writing in the same report, Professor Sir David Smithers was able to say: "We look ahead from the present, which is a good deal better than most people imagine. More progress producing real gains for cancer patients has occurred in the last decade or so than in any previous ten-year period."

Much – probably the greatest part – of that progress has been due to charity. Not only the general public but keen cancer charity workers often ask exactly what has been achieved. The latest available figures, produced at the end of 1973, tell a remarkable and heartening story. They show beyond all doubt that cancer is no longer the incurable killer, that today many who even ten years ago would have been dead are still alive and well. It is impossible to say how many people cancer research has saved from an untimely death, but look at the figures and remember that an improvement of only one or two per cent in any category may mean that thousands of lives have been saved.

The figures compare the percentage of people who were alive and well three years after the type of cancer from which they were suffering was diagnosed, and span a gap of 20 years. It is important to note that the statistics include cancers diagnosed at all stages. People who only went to their doctors when the disease was far advanced are included. *Survival rates are very much higher when cancer is diagnosed early.*

Cancer site	*Three-year survival rate for patients diagnosed 1949*	*Three-year survival rate for patients diagnosed 1969*	*Cancer site*	*Three-year survival rate for patients diagnosed 1949*	*Three-year survival rate for patients diagnosed 1969*
Bladder	48%	62%	Nose	30%	47%
Bone	34%	41%	Oesophagus	2%	5%
Brain	28%	37%	Ovary	30%	35%
Breast	63%	72%	Penis	59%	69%
Cervix	53%	63%	Pharynx	25%	32%
Colon	36%	50%	Prostate	49%	66%
Eye	77%	84%	Rectum	35%	49%
Gall-bladder	4%	11%	Salivary-gland	84%	89%
Hodgkin's Disease	35%	61%	Skin	49%	74%
Kidney	31%	44%	Stomach	12%	15%
Larynx	41%	54%	Testis	52%	69%
Leukaemia	0%	15%	Thyroid	67%	86%
Liver	7%	13%	Tongue	34%	41%
Lung	6%	11%	Vagina	30%	49%
Mouth	41%	51%	Vulva	56%	70%

It will be seen that the improvements in the survival rate extend from three per cent for cancers of the oesophagus and stomach to a dramatic 26 per cent for Hodgkin's Disease, and that at last progress is being made with leukaemia, invariably fatal in the past but with a survival rate of 15 per cent in 1969. Probably most of these statistics, maybe all of them, have improved since. For example, ln 1974 about 80 per cent of all cases of cancer of the cervix can be cured – compared with 63 per cent five years earlier – and very nearly 100 per cent are cured today if a pre-cancerous condition is detected by the cervical smear technique. If all women aged 25 and over would be screened regularly, this form of cancer could be almost eliminated, but despite all the publicity it has received many women do seem not to know about, or refuse to use the facilities available. The need for education, for which the charities have to raise so much money, is highlighted by the fact that even when they do find the services available, only about ten per cent of women respond spontaneously, 40 per cent have to be persuaded, and 50 per cent do not respond at all.

Unlike some other fields, there are only four major cancer charities in the United Kingdom and they certainly do not overlap in the accepted sense of the word. Two are devoted to research: the Imperial Cancer Research Fund, and the Cancer Research Campaign; two are concerned with relief, helping cancer sufferers in a number of ways: the Marie Curie Memorial Foundation, and the National Society for Cancer Relief. Among all four there is admittedly considerable competition for cash, but this chapter will show how differently they spend it. Each organization has its own adherents who almost certainly would not give money elsewhere. There are a number of small, local charities for cancer work of one kind and another and, laudable as they are, they do tend to confuse the picture. People have organized cancer appeals around the death of a relative or friend and often they would have been better advised to have first consulted the big four to ensure that the money raised is well spent. The costs of running a very small charity are almost always proportionately far greater than for a large one. All the major cancer organizations provide for individual trusts within their structures – money dedicated in the name of someone for a particular purpose.

The research societies have cross-membership of their scientific committees which allocate funds, the committees which decide on worthwhile projects, and this ensures that there is no waste but only co-ordination and a stronger common effort. The research organizations work in rather different ways towards the same end. While a future major breakthrough in cancer research is not impossible, most experts would say that solutions will only come through continued small advances in knowledge, each laboriously acquired by patient work in the laboratories. The funds are needed for equipment and, above all, for man and woman-power in the laboratories, hospitals and clinics. Like most charities, the cancer societies calculate that they have to increase their revenues by at least ten per cent each year just to keep up with inflation, let alone increase the scale of their work.

The largest and oldest research organization is the Imperial Cancer Research Fund, established in 1902 by the Royal College of Physicians of London and the Royal College of Surgeons of England at a time of great uncertainty and lack of any real knowledge of cancer. Work began in laboratories on London's Victoria Embankment, then in Queen Square, and from 1912 at Mill Hill. For years much of the direct research undertaken by the fund, as elsewhere, was concerned with studies of cancer in animals. The council of the Imperial fund decided in 1951 to place more emphasis on investigation of the disease in man, with research scientists working in the closest possible co-operation with physicians and surgeons in the great London hospitals. A small unit was started in Lincoln's Inn Fields and plans made to build a great new research centre. This cost £2.5m and was opened in 1962. All the money was raised by public subscription. Today it is one of the world's most important cancer research centres, where the staff includes biologists, pathologists, physiologists, virologists, pharmacologists, chemists and bio-chemists. The total staff is around 400, of which some 95 per cent are engaged purely in research, as distinct from administrative work. In fact the fund spends 95 per cent of all money raised directly on research.

Studies at the various laboratories at Lincoln's Inn Fields, Mill Hill, and in certain London hospitals include breast cancer, leukaemia, anti-tumour drugs, lung and prostate gland cancer, and viruses which may be a causative agent in some types of human cancer. The dilemma facing researchers is set out in one of the Imperial Cancer Research Fund's reports:

> In recent years the scope of cancer research has become increasingly ill-defined because, although the goal is obvious, the means of reaching it are not. Almost any biological and much chemical and physical research could have some bearing on the subject . . . One extreme view is that much could be done by the directed application of presently available knowledge and that most cancer research money should be concentrated on applying what we already know to cancer prevention, diagnosis and treatment. In other words, the aim should be for short-term gains.
>
> This country, for example, is even now faced with the tragic situation that most of the 30,000 deaths a year from lung cancer could be prevented by determined action to reduce smoking. Practical measures and applied research into the better use of existing drugs and improvements in methods of surgery and radiotherapy could save, or prolong, many lives in the immediate future. But these techniques are already so sophisticated that any dramatic improvements in their efficiency are unlikely and the majority of cancer cases will be unaffected.
>
> This leads to the other extreme argument: that the prevention or cure of most cancers will require an understanding of living systems which is going to take many decades of painstaking study to achieve and that the only sensible course is to get on with this basic research as fast as possible.

The Imperial Fund is striving to include both aims in its work. It is helped – as are so many other charities – by a number of contributing funds, by such organizations as the Variety Club of Great Britain, Rotary, Round Table, and Inner Wheel, by countless schools, colleges, women's organizations, churches, associations of all kinds and, quite considerably, by the collections made in public houses. House-to-house collections and flag days are held and the fund benefits each year from a very substantial investment income.

Among the most opulent headquarters of any charity is that of the Cancer Research Campaign in lordly Carlton House Terrace, overlooking the Mall and only yards from Buckingham and St James' palaces. There is a good reason for such splendour, as will be seen shortly. Unlike the Imperial – which tends to concentrate research in its own laboratories – Campaign undertakes very little actual research itself but makes grants to universities, hospitals, clinics and individuals throughout the country for approved projects. Currently it is supporting work in 19 institutions and giving grants to 93 individuals.

The year 1972 saw Campaign's golden jubilee, and revenue for the twelve months reached what its chairman, the Duke of Devonshire, described as the 'truly staggering' total of £3.8m, a rise of £1.2m on 1971 – though nearly half a million came from a single legacy. Commented the Duke: "It is particularly gratifying that such an outstanding result should have been obtained in the 50th year of our existence. This is no occasion for jubilation because, unlike a commercial company, we are trying to put ourselves out of business. Our target is to remove the very reason for our existence."

The Cancer Research Campaign was founded in 1922 at a time when – apart from the activities of the Imperial Fund, work at what was to become the Medical Research Council, and research at a number of different hospitals – there was no organization to bring the researchers together, to exchange information and ideas, or to provide funds for individual research. Some of the most famous men of the day, largely inspired by Mr J.P. Lockhart-Mummery, senior surgeon at St Mark's Hospital, met at the House of Commons, on the night of the budget debate, to found what was called the British Empire Cancer Campaign. They included Lord Dawson of Penn, then the King's Physician, Sir Thomas (later Lord) Horder, the celebrated pathologist, Sir Bernard Spilsbury, and the great criminal lawyer, Sir Edward Marshall-Hall. For years Campaign operated from the British

Red Cross Society offices. One of the first grants for research was to what is now the Royal Marsden Hospital. It was for £2,500. Today Campaign provides the Marsden's special research unit with no less than £350,000 a year.

Following the example of the Red Cross, Campaign set up a nation-wide network of local committees, which form the backbone of its fund-raising work today. In the early years, grants were made for research to various countries in the British Empire of the time but as the major countries set up their own associations, grants are made today only to Commonwealth countries with no substantial similar organizations of their own. The history of Campaign's fund-raising shows steady progress. In 1940 income was £35,000; in 1945 it was £111,000; in 1948 – silver jubilee year – it rose to £321,000. It was in 1961 that income topped £1m for the first time; the £2m mark was reached seven years later, and the £3m in golden jubilee year 1972.

In 1967 Mr (now Sir) Michael Sobell told the Duke of Devonshire that he would like to give him £500,000 for cancer work . . . "If you can tell me what you'd do with it!". He was told that one great desire was a joint headquarters for Campaign itself and the Royal College of Pathologists, who of course have much to do with cancer work. A long lease of the bombed-out Carlton House Terrace building was taken. Today the two organizations live there rent-free; they only have to pay rates and the electricity bill. Several other organizations are in a similar position – a move out of premises in central London, held on very long leases, or freehold, would lose them money.

Campaign now has some 800 local committees raising money for them, with 20 paid appeal secretaries who provide the link with the very small headquarters staff. They will go after money by almost any means, except football pools. One of the local committees' achievements has been accepted as a new record by the Guinness Book of Records! This was the collection in a Catford south-east London, pub of a pile of 1p and 2p coins totalling no less than £1,000.22 in 18 months. Still associated with beer but a rather different operation which benefited Campaign was Younger's Brewery Tartan Race from Edinburgh to London in 1973. Students took a fleet of gaily painted beer barrels, carried or propelled in all sorts of ways, to win £250 cash for the victor, £250 for a nominated charity, and of course some beer. The class for the most unconventional journey was won by a group from the West of Scotland Agricultural College, who transported their barrel on 'Tartanosaurus' – a combine harvester modified to look like a dinosaur! They not only nominated Cancer Research Campaign to receive the £250 but added £150 of their own cash prize.

Campaign money has gone to almost every kind of cancer research approved by the scientific committee since 1922. Among the few dramatic breakthroughs in cancer work that have been achieved with Campaign support was that at the Marsden, then the 'Royal Cancer Hospital', which in 1930 succeeded for the first time in identifying and isolating a pure chemical capable of producing cancer in the skin of mice, and this led in turn to the recognition of coal tar as a carcinogenic, or cancer-producing substance. Then there was the equally momentous success by Professor E.C. Dodds and his associates in synthesizing the highly active female sex hormone, stilboestrol, used now for the treatment of cancer of the prostate in men. In 1963 Dr M.A. Epstein and colleagues at Middlesex Hospital Medical School, again working with Campaign support, discovered what is now known as the Epstein Barr virus, one of the strongest candidates among those viruses suspected of causing some forms of human cancer. Campaign has sponsored much work on breast cancer and has established special tumour panels to aid early diagnosis of cancer. Research indicates – but has not yet finally proved – that it is likely that some forms of leukaemia, breast cancer and cancer of the cervix or womb may be caused by viruses. This, and much more, has all been done by charity.

Cancer Research Campaign's accounts for 1971 – a model of clarity and full information, incidentally – show that they raised £2.6m in that year, to be expended in 1972. They spent just over £3m on the main objects of the campaign, including £500,000 to establish a Chair of Clinical Oncology (cancer medical work which provides the link between the laboratory researchers and the clinicians) in the University of Manchester. They were able to spend more than £660,000 above their income because they knew revenue was rising. Administration and staff expenses accounted for only 2.23 per cent of income. Apart from direct grants to others and establishing chairs of cancer medicine, Campaign has now started its own laboratory at Nottingham University for work in tumour immunology.

Campaign, like some other charities as we have seen, is occasionally used by crooks! Representatives of certain types of trading companies call at homes and say "We give a third of all proceeds to the Cancer Research Campaign." If asked for proof – which is rare – they produce a genuine receipt for a donation to Campaign . . . but nobody can tell of what sum this is 'a third' or even if it is the one and only donation the company has made to any cancer organization. Every genuine collector, for any charity, should be able to produce authentication.

The National Society for Cancer Relief celebrated its diamond jubilee in 1971. This society does not contribute largely to research, though it does make some grants here. Its main function is the direct alleviation of suffering, to provide food and clothing, proper nursing, convalesence, transport, comforts of various kinds and fares for relations and friends to visit cancer patients in hospitals and nursing homes. It contributes to a number of cancer homes, both with annual grants and with capital sums to help build or improve them.

In 1953 the society had a total income of £76,608, of which legacies accounted for £33,102. Expenditure on benefits in that year was £46,100, to 4,496 cases. In 1972 income was £742,472, of which legacies came to £325,613. Direct relief expenditure was £426,003, to 11,777 cases. General administration cost 3.13 per cent and the cost of administration of benefit payments was a further two per cent of income. The society's assets rose from £688,937 in 1970 to just over £1m.

They operate throughout England, Scotland and Wales, all Ireland and the Channel Islands, and can be seen very clearly to meet needs not covered by the Welfare State, providing not only money and nursing home accommodation, but also items like an electric page-turner for a paralysed cancer patient and food liquidizers for people who have had operations for cancer of the throat.

The Marie Curie Memorial Foundation was set up in 1948 to establish its own residential homes throughout the country for cancer patients, to provide nursing and other help for patients in their own homes, and to organize an advisory service for the general public on certain aspects of cancer. They have 12 homes, of which one is in London, three in Scotland, one in Wales and one in Belfast. Patients are invited to contribute to their maintenance costs but financial hardship is never permitted to affect admission or after-care. Under a welfare grant scheme, help is brought to many cancer patients being nursed at home, help that can often otherwise be delayed by administrative processes or bureaucracy. Block grants are made to local medical officers of health, from which district nurses may draw to buy *immediately* things needed by patients which are not met from other sources. There is a day and night nursing service, administered by the medical officers of health but paid for by the Foundation, a scheme whereby 'sitters' can be provided so that relatives of cancer patients may secure rest and recreation, and a specialist rehabilitation service to restore incapacitated patients and enable them to work and enjoy independence. The Foundation has a research establishment of its own at Limpsfield, Surrey.

The 1971/72 report of the Foundation recorded income of £1,064,821 and expenditure of £1,047,041, indicating the struggle with the ever-increasing costs of commodities and remuneration of nursing and domestic staff. The cost of running the 12 homes rose from £569,072 to £643,748, and 2,333 patients were admitted during the year, an increase of 103. More than 5,000 patients were helped by the welfare and night nursing service and the cost of this rose by almost £25,000, though the Department of Health and Social Security provided the Foundation with £25,000 a year for three years to help expand the service. Research expenditure rose from £86,129 to £123,592.

Of the patients admitted to Foundation homes – with 409 beds at the time – there were two women for every man; ages ranged from 20 to over 90, with by far the greatest number in the 60-79 age-group. The average total cost per patient per week increased in the year from £30.57 to £33.07. The average weekly contribution from patients rose from £9.18 to £11.95.

Apart from the enormous volume of voluntary work, both in fund-raising and visiting patients in their own or the Foundation's homes, more than 700 people are fully employed and their aggregate remuneration during 1971/72 came to £635,495. All in all, though the Foundation's income rose by 14 per cent, expenditure increased by 20 per cent.

Those sort of figures emphasize the main problem of charity organizations which operate homes of any kind and have to maintain staff to run them.

19

'A MERCY WHICH DOES NOT QUAIL'

"*It drives on with a mercy which does not quail in the presence of death; it drives on as a proof, a symbol, a testimony that man is created in the image of God and that valour and virtue have not perished in the British race.*"

So said Winston Churchill of the lifeboat when, in 1924, he was at a celebration of the centenary of the Royal National Lifeboat Institution, an extraordinary and truly unique charitable association. It is unique in that it is the only charity in Britain which fulfils and pays for all the work that falls within its sphere . . . and it is quite often criticized just for this! The complaint is that life-saving should not be left to charity, but should be the responsibility of the Government or at the very least of some sort of shipping organization since it is the shipping industry that is – erroneously – considered to benefit most from the existence of the R.N.L.I.

The Institution has been running with supreme efficiency for 150 years and it would be freely admitted in Whitehall that no Government in Britain could afford to do the job so well. Between 1854 and 1869 the Institution did in fact come to some degree under Government control as it received a grant to help it out of serious financial difficulties. But when Governments give money they always impose conditions; there are invariably strings! After 15 years of a degree of State interference, the Institution decided to become fully independent again and has remained so ever since. Before the last war, Germany had a voluntary lifeboat service and, after a short period of State control, reverted to the old system. Sweden has a voluntary system also while the Netherlands has two charity services: the South Holland Lifeboat Association and the North and South Holland Lifeboat Association.

Under a State system, service in lifeboats would have to be full-time and that would practically kill off Britain's fishing industry, since so many lifeboat men are also fishermen and the industry is short enough of man-power already. A State system would be thoroughly wasteful because the 'full-time' men would be sitting around for days, sometimes for weeks, doing nothing productive. As for the suggestion that the lifeboat service should be financed by shipping companies, many such companies are registered overseas and it would be impossible to collect any sort of charge from them. Nor would it be desirable to impose a levy on yachtsmen and the other small-boat users who make continually increasing demands on the R.N.L.I. these days, since this would have to be by a Government tax, and, as we all know, Governments dislike applying taxes to specific purposes – consider the old Road Fund!

A House of Commons committee studied the question of an independent lifeboat service towards the end of the last century and decided that there were no grounds for changing the system. Through both World Wars, when the need was at its peak, successive Governments remained convinced that the voluntary way was best.

The R.N.L.I. exists entirely on freely given money, largely raised by some 2,000 fund-gathering branches in Britain and Eire, where the R.N.L.I. also operate the lifeboats. Its 200 stations round the 5,000 miles of British and Irish coasts, with about 250 boats of various kinds, today make about 2,000 launches a year – compared with 300 or so in the 1930s – and save an average of more than 100 lives every month. The annual bill for all this now comes to around £3m, and that is apart from capital expenditure.

Ever since its foundation in 1824, the reigning British monarch has been patron of the R.N.L.I. and since 1900 a member of the Royal Family has been president. Today the Duke of Kent is president. Britain was the first country in the world to have a national lifeboat institution and was closely followed by the Netherlands. Many lifeboat societies to be formed later in other countries were modelled on the R.N.L.I. In some countries, such as the United States of America, where the service is part of the Coast Guard, there is State control, in others it remains voluntary.

The first lifeboat station in Britain – and probably in the world – was established in the late eighteenth century at Bamburgh, Northumberland, the birthplace of Grace Darling. A charitable trust, known as the Crewe Trust, was set up at Bamburgh Castle after the death in 1721 of the third Baron Crewe, Bishop of Durham, and appears to have operated an elaborate organization for providing help in cases of shipwreck. In 1786 the chief administrator of the trust contacted Lionel Lukin, a London coachbuilder and prolific inventor. He had been carrying out experiments with a yawl to give it more buoyancy and make it, in his own words, 'unimmergible'. Lukin converted a small cobble which served for some years at Bamburgh, so he may be said to have been the inventor of the lifeboat. After the wreck of a ship near the mouth of the Tyne in 1789, a social club known as the Gentlemen of the Lawe House offered a prize of two guineas for the best design of a rescue vessel. The winner was William Wouldhave, parish clerk of South Shields, and his design, modified by members of the adjudicating committee, was the basis on which Henry Greathead, a South Shields boatbuilder, constructed the *Original*, the first boat in the world to be designed and built as a lifeboat. Launched in 1790, she remained in service for 40 years.

From the very start then, it can be seen that lifeboats were founded in charity. Greathead built more than 30 of them, all paid for by private money, in many cases by Lloyds. These were manned and administered locally. Then, in 1823, Sir William Hillary published in Douglas, Isle of Man, a pamphlet entitled 'An Appeal to the British Nation on the Humanity and Policy of forming a National Institution for the Preservation of Lives and Property from Shipwreck'. Hillary was a regular member of the lifeboat crew at Douglas, where a station had been established in 1802. A year after his appeal he met Thomas Wilson, one of the Members of Parliament for the City of London, who was the prime mover behind a meeting presided over by the then Archbishop of Canterbury, Dr Manners Sutton, in the City on 4 March 1824. Here the 'National Institution for the Preservation of Life from Shipwreck' was launched and 30 years later it became the Royal National Lifeboat Institution. Thirteen years after its foundation, the 'Shipwreck Institution', as it was popularly known, had an annual income of only about £250. There were at the start about 40 lifeboats, propelled by sails or oars or both. The principles of organization and administration have remained relatively unchanged through 150 years of experience. The committee of management has always included men of distinction in many fields, who give their services free. Stations are controlled by voluntary local committees with an honorary secretary handling the administration and, generally, taking the decision on whether or not to launch the lifeboat. Apart from a remarkably small central administrative staff at the Institution's headquarters, a total of 98, there are some 25 technical personnel such as inspectors of lifeboats, engineers, hull surveyors, and nine organizing secretaries who co-ordinate the money-raising throughout Britain and Ireland.

Over its 150 years' history the highlights of development in this service can be listed as follows: the adoption of a self-righting boat following a design competition in 1851; the first steam lifeboat in 1890; the first petrol engine in a lifeboat in 1904; use of radio telephony in 1929; the diesel engine in 1932; twin-screw engines for the smallest boats in 1936; construction of the Oakley self-righting boat in 1958; and the introduction of the inshore rescue boat in 1963.

It is a story of a never-ending battle to increase the range, power, strength and efficiency of lifeboats but it has not been so much of a battle to pay for it all. For the public response always seems to rise to the needs of the day. The history is studded with tales of gallantry, the 'mercy which does not quail', but perhaps the best example of the spirit animating the R.N.L.I. was the famous and all but incredible rescue in Porlock Bay. It was a January night in 1899 and the lifeboat at Lynmouth, Devon, could not be launched to a ship in distress in the bay because a westerly gale was sweeping seas right across the harbour and over the front. To reach the ship, the Lynmouth crew and a number of volunteer helpers, with horses, transported their lifeboat *13 miles overland*. They had to take the boat from sea level to a height of 1,400 feet, much of the way up a gradient of one in 4½. They had to dig down banks, knock down gateposts, break down walls and cut down trees. Their only lights were oil lamps that were continually blown out by the gale sweeping across Exmoor. After a 10½ hours' journey they launched the boat from Porlock, into the gale, without even pausing to eat, and safely reached the ship in distress.

The R.N.L.I. fleet consists today of 134 conventional lifeboats and 118 inshore lifeboats, ranging in size from 17 to 71 feet. There is also a reserve fleet of 57 boats. Many of these boats are named after the people and organizations who gave money or left legacies sufficient to pay for a complete boat. The conventional lifeboats vary in size and some other respects, according to launching conditions at the station from which they operate. All new lifeboats being built now will right themselves automatically if they capsize. The inshore lifeboats were about 16 feet in length when first brought into service in 1963, inflatable and constructed of tough nylon. Driven by a 40 h.p. motor, they can reach a speed of about 25 knots. The normal crew is two and they seldom need more than two other helpers to launch them. They are specially designed for work close inshore during the summer months and there are now more than 100 inshore stations – which save more lives than the conventional boats because of the growth of pleasure boating of all kinds. In addition to all this, the R.N.L.I. operates, in conjunction with the Coast Guard service, the 'inshore rescue scheme'. Private boats take part in this if they are suitable and generally available when needed and the R.N.L.I. pays rewards to the crews of these vessels on the same scale as to regular lifeboat men.

The Institution never has any difficulty in getting lifeboat crews – it is an honour to serve in them. Normally there is only one full-time servant of the R.N.L.I. at each lifeboat station, the motor mechanic, who is responsible for seeing that the boat is ready to put to sea at any moment. The rest of the crew earn their livings in other ways. A huge proportion of them are fishermen, of course, and in some stations it has been the tradition for years and years that fishermen provide the entire crew. This is the case for instance at Whitby, the station which has won the R.N.L.I.'s gold medal, its highest award for gallantry, more times than any other place. Elsewhere crewmen may be local tradesmen, builders, printers (there is at least one verger), while Lord Mottistone, one-time Secretary of State for War, served in an Isle of Wight lifeboat crew for more than 40 years. The development of the inshore boats has brought in more professional men – bankers, doctors, lawyers and the like. The coxswain, second coxswain and some others of a lifeboat crew may sometimes receive small retaining fees but all members of the crew are paid at the rate of two pounds for the first two hours plus 50p for each additional hour when they go out on service, or £1.75 for a three-hour exercise. It is not a princely sum. In the conventional lifeboats the crew normally consists of seven, including men qualified in first aid, radio and signalling.

The equipment on a modern lifeboat is far more sophisticated than in the early days, and much more costly. It includes medium frequency radio telephony for contact with the shore or other vessels, and V.H.F. or U.H.F. radio for talking with aircraft, notably helicopters with which the lifeboats carry out regular joint exercises. Then there are loud-hailers, floodlights, searchlights, signalling lamps, line-throwing pistols, direction-finding gear, echo sounders, oil for smoothing the water around a wreck, first-aid kits, stretchers, axes, flares, sometimes radar. There have been times when a lifeboat was called to a rescue on dry land! The coxswain of the Clovelly lifeboat was told by Hartland Point Coastguard that the lifeboat station's honorary medical adviser was attending an elderly woman who had collapsed in Clovelly's main street. She was in urgent need of oxygen until the arrival of an ambulance. The doctor had no oxygen equipment with him but he knew the lifeboat had. An inshore lifeboat, carried on board the main boat, rushed the equipment to shore and a lifeboat man ran with it to the doctor, who was able to sustain the casualty until the arrival of the ambulance.

An analysis of the work of the R.N.L.I. in the year 1971 shows that conventional lifeboats were called out on service 1,165 times and inshore boats 1,511. The main boats saved 662 lives. The total number saved by all R.N.L.I. services was 1,722, which brought the grand aggregate between 4 March 1824 and 3 December 1971 to 94,923. (By December 1973 it was 98,364.)

Of the lives saved by the big boats in 1971, the greatest percentage, 41.2, was from commercial fishing vessels, 19.8 per cent from sailing pleasure craft, 2.6 per cent from 'row boats', 2.3 per cent from foreign-going merchant vessels, 2.2 per cent from home trade merchant vessels, 1.5 per cent from naval vessels, and 1.3 per cent from boring rigs. Lives saved by inshore vessels included 39.8 per cent from sailing pleasure craft, 28.7 per cent from powered pleasure craft, 14.4 per cent people stranded or fallen off cliffs, and 11.2 per cent from manually propelled pleasure craft. Other rescues included relieving lighthouses, helping aircraft, taking out doctors, and rescuing bathers, skin-divers and animals.

To do all this the R.N.L.I. raises money in almost every way it can – except through professional fund-raisers, in whom it does not believe! There are house-to-house collections – no commissions are paid – flag days, coffee mornings, events running from full-scale charity balls and fashion shows to small local whist drives and jumble sales. Advertising is kept on a fairly modest scale and is of the nature of a 'reminder' only. Understandably, the Institution finds it easiest to raise money where people have a connection with the sea – it is not so easy in the Midlands for example. Every year Scotland raises more money per head of the population that the rest of Britain and Ireland – after all, virtually every city and town of Scotland has some connection with the sea. Unlike most United Kingdom charities, the Institution does get some money from foreign countries. For example, if a Greek or Italian ship is saved the owners may send a donation. The big insurance companies also give to the R.N.L.I. which is only fair! And money pours in after a lifeboat disaster or a spectacular rescue. Many commercial firms help the R.N.L.I. Once the lifeboats carried rum, strictly for medicinal use. Today they have a free supply of Martell brandy, and still with stern control on consumption. When this first became known there were objections from some temperance enthusiasts who claimed that the Institution was helping to promote the booze trade!

The R.N.L.I. does a great deal of promotional work among children and here it is helped immensely by the BBC and ITV. When some years ago the BBC's *Blue Peter* programme appealed for paperback books to be sold for inshore lifeboats, they received a quarter of a million. The boats for which they paid are now called 'Blue Peter boats'. On another occasion when *Blue Peter* announced a competition for the design of a lifeboat flag day poster, there were 80,000 entries.

The R.N.L.I. can claim to have invented flag days. In the 1880s it was found that two-thirds of the Institution's regular income came every year from about a hundred people. Sir Charles Macara, a Lancashire businessman, inaugrated in Manchester the type of street collection which became known as Lifeboat Saturday. Once again it was a case of what Manchester does today . . . This was in October 1891. There was a procession, including lifeboats, three bands and fire and ambulance detachments. Money was thrown from windows and the tops of trams into the collecting carts and more than £600 was raised, mostly in coppers. The lifeboats were later launched into an artificial lake and a rescue by rocket apparatus was watched by 30,000 people. The actual sale of paper flags began in 1915 and flag days now provide about 15 per cent of the Institution's income.

Compared with many charities the R.N.L.I.'s annual accounts are veritable models of honesty and clarity. The 1971 accounts shown an increase in total expenditure from £2,186,000 in 1970 to £2,566,000. Income rose by £196,000 to £2,501,380. But there was also a profit on the sale of investments and an appreciation in the value of the remainder, which meant a net increase of £753,029 in the reserve for capital expenditure. There are some charities which only record investments and properties at original cost price whatever may have happened in the intervening years!

R.N.L.I. capital expenditure – new and replacement boats and equipment, etc. – rose by £175,000 to £546,000 in 1971. Recurrent expenditure increased from £1,850,000 to £2,009,000. For the first time the R.N.L.I. branches and women's guilds raised more than a million pounds, while legacies for general purposes came to £882,219 (£820,297 in 1970). Gifts and legacies for special purposes were £449,890 (£523,054). During the year the Civil Service and Post Office Lifeboat Fund provided no less than £38,000, while Alexander Duckham and Company undertook to provide lubricating oils free for the Institution's fleet. Of all expenditure during the year, £1,161,845 went directly on the lifeboat service, including £430,789 on maintenance and development, and £327,359 to crews. Central administration costs were £366,567, while fund-raising cost £458,386 and advertising and exhibitions £22,917. The total assets of the Institution at the end of the year were £3,816,569.

Two quite different examples of rescue work during the year may be chosen to illustrate the R.N.L.I.'s work. In June the inshore lifeboat at Barmouth, Merionethshire, was asked to help a badly injured woman who had fallen from cliffs at Friog. As there was a force seven wind with heavy rain squalls, the main lifeboat was also launched. Dr Robert A. Haworth, a regular crew member, joined the rescue team. The woman had fallen over cliffs about 80 feet high and though there were two policemen and a mountain rescue expert with her, it was impossible to get her up the cliff because of the overhang. The beach was being covered by the rising tide and there was only about 25 feet in width left exposed.

It was decided to 'charge' the beach in the small inshore boat, through the rain squalls, sea mist, a ten-foot high swell running obliquely to the beach, and spray being thrown some 25 feet into the air as the sea hit boulders up to six feet in diameter on the beach and at the foot of the cliffs. The boat approached at speed, cut its engines, and after hitting some of the big boulders, landed on the beach. The crew had to drag the boat to safety while the doctor attended to the woman, who was in a serious state. As it would have taken about four hours to get a stretcher up the cliff, it was decided to take the woman off in the boat, which was re-launched with great difficulty and taken to a nearby cove where conditions were better, though the two men manning the boat had to wade shoulder-high in water to land the boat on the second beach.

The woman was carried from cove to cove over rocks, strapped to the mountain rescue stretcher and covered with a plastic bag. The men had to wade shoulder-high into the sea once more to get the vessel into deep enough water to start the engine, but they succeeded. The woman was taken to a sandy beach at Friog. The whole rescue had taken only 40 minutes from the boat's arrival on the scene, but the woman died five hours later. In addition to letters of appreciation to the crew of the main lifeboat – which had stood by throughout the rescue – and of thanks to the people on the beach, the R.N.L.I. awarded its silver medal to every member of the inshore boat's crew, including, of course, the doctor.

In November, during a force ten wind gusting to force 12 – top of the Beaufort scale – the 70-foot steel lifeboat *Grace Paterson Ritchie* fought a four and a half hour battle in the harbour of Kirkwall in the Orkneys to save four Danish fishing vessels which had broken from their pier moorings. One of them was aground. Working with coast guards, the lifeboat crew got ropes to all four ships in succession until all were safe and the lives of 20 fishermen were preserved. The insurance underwriters of the vessels considered that the lifeboat prevented more than £100,000 worth of damage to the ships and made a voluntary payment of £500 to the R.N.L.I. itself and £500 to the lifeboat's crew, though no salvage claim was made or even anticipated. The lifeboat coxswain was awarded the Institution's bronze medal and the rest of the crew received certificates.

It could be said to have been just routine.

20

CRADLE, KENNEL, AND NATURE RESERVE

Sometimes people assert that Britain loves her dogs and cats, even nature conservation projects, more than her children, and donates more money to the 50 or so animal and 'preservation' charities than to young humans, although in 1973 more than half a million unwanted cats and dogs had to be destroyed and if anything litter and vandalism in the countryside has got worse in many places. In fact, while Britain does do more relatively for animals and 'nature' generally than any other country, she can be said to care – in financial terms – three times as much for children!

Taking the top 50 organizations only, here are the incomes from gifts and legacies in 1971 to charities in the two groups:

	Children			*Animals & Nature*	
(2)	Dr Barnardo's Homes	£2,874,000	(12)	R.S.P.C.A.	£1,659,000
(9)	Save the Children Fund	£2,388,000	(19)	National Trust	£1,106,000
(13)	C. of E. Children's Society	£1,457,000	(35)	World Wildlife Foundation	£ 445,000
(15)	N.S.P.C.C.	£1,389,000			£3,210,000
(18)	National Children's Home	£1,107,000			
(47)	Scout Association	£ 291,000			
(50)	National Society for Mentally Handicapped Children	£ 280,000			
		£9,784,000			

(*Numbers in brackets denote place in the 'league table'*)

If one progresses to a study of the next 50 charities, a further £380,000 for animals would have to be added – for Blue Cross (62 in the 'league') and the Royal Society for the Protection of Birds (64). Against that must be set, however, some £587,000 – ranging from totals of £197,000 down to £53,000 – received by the Y.M.C.A. (63), Shaftesbury

Society (78), Invalid Children's Association (81), National Association of Boys' Clubs (85), Boys' Brigade (87), Y.M.C.A. (88), and National Association of Youth Clubs (95). So the children still win. But it is arguable whether all these are strictly 'children's' charities. There is obviously considerable difficulty in drawing rigid descriptive lines here.

Oldest of all children's charities are the Shaftesbury Homes, founded in 1843, and the Shaftesbury Society, set up the following year as the 'Ragged School Union'. In all there are more than 70 organizations of varying kinds, including voluntary youth work associations such as the Boys' Brigade, young farmers' clubs, and youth hostels associations, to name but a few.

After Dr Barnardo's, the National Society for the Prevention of Cruelty to Children is the best-known and most important organization working for children in Britain, since the Save the Children Fund operates predominantly overseas, in some 50 countries. In Britain it provides homes, clubs and playgroups.

Founder of the N.S.P.C.C. was Benjamin Waugh, born in the Yorkshire village of Settle in 1839, the son of a saddler. He became a Congregational minister after studying at a theological college in Bradford, where he was described as being 'as ready to battle with his professors as he was with his fellow students'. He came to work in East Greenwich, London, around 1868, among the worst slum areas of the day. Like Dr Barnardo at much the same time, he was appalled by the sight of children begging in the streets, by the thousands of babies who died through over-laying. It was a time when parents could do what they liked with their children, the law had no power to help, and baby farming, as well as the practice of insuring the lives of infants who were then murdered, were rampant. The law was powerless to protect these children but it was ruthless in dealing with child offenders and in 1873 Waugh wrote a famous book *The Gaol Cradle: Who rocks it*? Every magistrate in England received a copy of this book, in which Waugh pleaded for special children's courts. He established a *crêche* where mothers could leave their children when going out to work and set up a system under which he went bail for children summoned at Greenwich Police Court. He would then provide them with employment such as selling boot polish or collecting waste paper for sale. The Greenwich magistrates came to send so many children to Waugh instead of prison that he decided to form a society specially for their protection. More than anything else he sought to change the law to give children certain basic rights, but the climate of opinion was not ready for that. In 1881 the Reverend George Staite, Vicar of Ashton Hayes, Cheshire, wrote to the *Liverpool Mercury*: "Whilst we have a Society for the Prevention of Cruelty to Animals can we not do something to prevent cruelty to children?" Staite wrote also to Lord Shaftesbury, who replied: "The evils you state are enormous and indisputable, but they are of so private, internal and domestic a character as to be beyond the reach of legislation, and the subject indeed would not I think be entertained in either House of Parliament."

America also had an organisation for animal welfare before it had one for children but a New York Society for the Prevention of Cruelty to Children was formed in 1875, with the help of Henry Bergh, founder of the New York animals' society. In 1881 a Liverpool banker named Agnew visited a number of child protection societies that had by then been formed in the United States and on his return home founded in 1883 the Liverpool Society for the Prevention of Cruelty to Children. Agnew was invited to London and met Waugh. On 8 July 1884 the London Society was formed at a meeting in the Mansion House, which was attended among others, by Lord Shaftesbury, the Baroness Burdett Coutts, Cardinal Manning and Dr Barnardo. Lord Shaftesbury was elected president and Waugh honorary secretary and later director. As the American animal society had helped its children's society, so did the British one, for early meetings of the N.S.P.C.C. committee were held in the board room of the R.S.P.C.A. in Jermyn Street, Mayfair.

Waugh launched *The Child's Guardian* magazine in 1887, in which he was to write later words that have remained a guiding principle of the N.S.P.C.C. throughout its existence: "It is better to remove the evil from the home than remove the child."

By 1889 a total of 31 aid committees had been established throughout England and they united to form the National Society. Branches were opened in Dublin, Belfast and Cork and they operated under the N.S.P.C.C. until 1956, when an Irish Society took over. A Scottish National Society was formed in 1899 and in 1922 received a Royal Charter as the Royal Scottish Society for the Prevention of Cruelty to Children – securing a 'Royal' prefix still lacked by the N.S.P.C.C.! The original 31 aid committees now number more than 200 and form the backbone of the N.S.P.C.C.

In 1889 also, Queen Victoria became patron of the N.S.P.C.C. and the Children's Charter, the Act for the Prevention of Cruelty to Children, was passed by Parliament, largely due to the work of the society. Other Acts extending protection to children were to follow in 1894 and 1904. The society received a Royal Charter in May, 1895, defining its duties as 'To prevent the public and private wrongs of children'.

The condition of many children at the time the N.S.P.C.C. began was indeed atrocious. Almost a century later, in May 1971, Sir Keith Joseph, as Secretary of State for Social Services, addressed the society's council. Referring to a 'veritable avalanche of social need', he added: "The more we look at this catalogue of misery the more it is mad to contemplate that the State can tackle it all – it cannot."

To take that year 1971, the N.S.P.C.C. investigated no less than 24,395 new cases in England, Wales and Northern Ireland. They helped an average of 1,400 children each week, 40 per cent of them under five years of age. The society is sometimes thought of as merely a 'prosecuting' body, but of all the investigations undertaken in the year there were only 43 prosecutions, in which 53 people were convicted. Eleven of these were given suspended sentences and 21 placed on probation. Just over 12,000 of all cases were brought to the society by parents themselves and 4,693 arose from reports from the general public, with a further 6,000 or so from various officials. During the year 2,146 children were found to be well cared for and there was consequently no case; 3,594 lacked physical care; 898 were physically injured; 2,658 were emotionally disturbed; 57,148 were listed as 'at risk but without symptom at present'; 2,183 were not living at home. Causes included 8,443 cases of 'serious disharmony between parents', 6,090 cases in which there was only one parent, 4,554 cases of mental or emotional disability in the family, 1,589 in which one or both parents came from outside the United Kingdom, 6,741 serious financial problems, and 3,392 cases of unsatisfactory housing.

Behind all those statistics, how do the N.S.P.C.C.'s 320 or so men and women officers carry on their work of helping about 80,000 children a year today? Just what do they do and what do they see? The work includes dealing with cases of physical or mental cruelty to children and long-term neglect, providing advice and help on request – around 49 per cent of all cases in a typical year – and undertaking research, for example into battered children, drink and drugs, isolation in high-rise flats, and the allocations of space to children in new home developments.

More than 4,000 babies are battered each year in Britain, according to the latest statistics, and up to 18 per cent of them die. Reports on a group of battered babies studied in Midland hospitals showed that one-third were illegitimate and almost half were conceived before marriage. The average age of mothers was 23 and fathers 27. Many had been battered themselves as children.

One of the society's annual reports described a day in the diary of an N.S.P.C.C. inspector. Here are parts of it.

> 8.30 a.m. Mrs A telephones to say her nine-year-old daughter Amy did not return home last night. I contact police and her school, saying I will ring back later. Will keep my eye out for her during the day. I remember when this happened once before I found her at 2.00 a.m. in a telephone kiosk . . .
>
> I can get out at about 9.45 a.m. Call on Mrs B aged 37, who is severely disabled with muscular dystrophy. She always has great difficulty in getting to the door to open it. Have recently managed to get a telephone installed so that she can order her shopping and have some contact with other people. She is married to a schizophrenic who once drove her to the country, beat her up and left her to get home as best she could. She is now divorcing him but until the divorce comes through the Council will not transfer the home to her name, so she worries constantly he will throw her out of the home. She manages her two sons well though, seeing that they get out to Scouts, a Youth Club, and so on. She worries about everything but her sense of humour always amazes me.
>
> On to the C family living in two rooms in a multi-occupied house. Last time I was here the hall and landing were crowded with dustbins and litter, dogs running wild and the one bathroom out of order. Find that the Council have been in and done a good cleaning job. Mrs C is preparing lunch; she is young, slim and pretty and smiles easily. He is difficult and unresponsive. Says he has been looking for a job. Must get them out of this house. Matrimonial problems – she married to get away from home. The living room has a kitchen table, two chairs and a sofa, old-fashioned sink in the corner with cold water tap only. (Can't think how she manages.) The room is heated by the oven with the door left open. The toddler and the baby in the pram are also in the room together with a guinea pig in a cage, a budgie, a cat and a goldfish. The children are well cared-for and fit but there is a hopelessness about their lives. Will ring the housing department again when I get back . . .
>
> Stop at telephone box to contact police. They tell me Amy has

turned up at school. That's a relief. After a quick lunch I collect Amy's mother from her tower block flat and drive her to the school, only to find Amy has been allowed out after school with the other girls and is missing again. Drive mother home. On the way to my last call I see Amy walking hand in hand with a friend. I bundle them both into the car. Amy says she spent the night at this girl's home. I tell her how worried her mother has been and she begs me to come into the flat with her. I do so and stay with them until the situation has calmed down. This is the typical problem of an immigrant family: the parents coming to this country, leaving the children with their grand-parents and then sending for them after five or six years. Amy and her parents are almost strangers to each other.

Among major worries for the society is the number of cases of children left alone while their parents go out, sometimes with fatal results. One N.S.P.C.C. annual report quoted a case where less than 48 hours after a mother had been warned about neglecting her two-year-old son, he died in a fire while both parents were out drinking. The parents were prosecuted for neglect and fined £50. The same annual report recorded a sordidly vivid example of the kind of case with which the society has to deal. The N.S.P.C.C. were called in because of a report that twins aged three-and-a-half were being severely neglected. The inspector's notes read: "... The twins were in a bedroom which smelt worse than an open sewer. It was impossible to walk in the room without treading on excreta; the walls were also covered in it. There were 72 empty milk bottles in the kitchen. The house was filthy, except for the sitting room, which was clean, with a television and a large radiogram in the room."

Those children were committed to the care of the local authority. The parents were prosecuted ... and both placed on probation. Comment on both court decisions seems superfluous.

The society runs therapeutic playgroups, even in troubled Northern Ireland, where the work is done under great difficulties. They provide cash in certain situations, such as a crisis where immediate help can prevent a complete disaster, like the break-up of a family, and they distribute hundreds of items of clothing and furniture in a year. Each year too they send hundreds of children for seaside holidays and they give presents and parties to thousands every Christmas.

Money for all this is raised by more than 200 branches and 5,000 local committees, forming a body of about 65,000 honorary supporters, and an important part of the society's income comes from children themselves, through the League of Pity and its Blue Egg savings boxes. Money is raised in schools, by sponsored events, and by plain ingenuity and enthusiasm on the part of the children.

However, legacies have been the largest single source of income for the society for many years and in 1971 they reached a record total of £444,525 – see the R.S.P.C.A. figure later! Of the society's general income for the year, totalling £962,908, subscriptions and donations accounted for £250,750, local authority grants £24,495, various fund-raising events £301,460, and the League of Pity £84,177. Expenditure reached £1,288,139, of which £896,568 went directly on case-work services and £102,416 on educational and advisory publicity, a vital part of this society's function. Administration expenses totalled £61,657.

All that means that it cost about 5p a day to help every child coming to the notice of the N.S.P.C.C.

Of recent years the Royal Society for the Prevention of Cruelty to Animals has hit the headlines more often because of internal warfare than through its welfare work! Nevertheless the society does invaluable work not only for household pets, strays and so forth, but as watchdog over animal experimentation, intensive animal husbandry systems, export of animals for slaughter, the welfare of horses and the protection of seals. Statistics again: the society maintains more than 60 animal homes and nearly 80 clinics, four hospitals, four mobile units, and more than 100 welfare centres. In 1971 the number of animals treated rose to 290,535 from 242,645 the previous year. A total of 281,959 animals were humanely destroyed and new homes were found for 69,763 luckier ones – 39,000 of them dogs. Out of 26,043 complaints investigated, verbal cautions were given in 4,416 cases, 19 offenders were jailed, there were 23 juvenile convictions and 255 people were disqualified from keeping animals for varying periods.

When one considers the relatively light fines and the incidence of probation sentences in child cruelty or neglect cases, it is interesting to look at the sort of penalties secured by the R.S.P.C.A. for animal offences. Penalties in specimen court cases quoted in the 1971 annual report included £50 fine and £24.20 costs for ill-treating 14 dogs, £50 and £16 costs for neglect of two mongrel puppies, £50 fine and £50 costs for neglecting six horses, and £50 fine and £33.90 costs for causing suffering to a yearling colt.

As part of its constant and often controversial activities in all possible aspects of animal welfare – including fox-hunting, bull-fighting, performing animals, horse-racing and zoos – the society provides lecturers for schools and youth clubs, and a whole range of audio-visual aids ranging from warning films to wall charts and colour films and slides on pet care.

At the end of 1971 the society had total assets of £4,266,910, of which investments represented some £3.5m. Aggregate income received at headquarters for the year was £647,477 plus no less than £1.4m in legacies, or more than three times the amount left the in the same year to the N.S.P.C.C.! Operating expenditure totalled £1,280,662 (£1,130,316 in 1970). Of this, the inspectorate service cost £537,371, prosecutions £30,203, and regional organization £58,475. The costs of education and appeals are lumped together at £193,280 – which one thinks perhaps should not happen – and clinics and homes cost £312,853. Administration costs were an additional £179,068.

Legacies again play a major role in the income of the Blue Cross, which runs an animal hospital in Victoria, London, as well as cat shelters and dogs' homes and rest fields for old donkeys in various parts of the country. Blue Cross got £91,000 in legacies in 1960, rising to £147,000 out of an income of £199,000 – excluding rents and investment income – in 1971. "People think that animals cannot look after themselves . . . there is no Welfare State for animals", said Mr Peter Arpmael, Blue Cross's director.

When it comes to the lower end, financially, of the animal charities scale, generally people who see those Victorian horse troughs to be found in London and other places have no idea that the Metropolitan Drinking Fountain and Cattle Trough Association, founded in 1859, is still very much in being, though its £4,000 or so annual income comes almost entirely from past investments. In 1970 it received just £38 in subscriptions and donations. What does it find to do in this motor age? Each year it provides about 50 drinking fountains . . . for thirsty humans, mainly in the Greater London area. These go into children's playgrounds, recreation grounds and parks. To preserve its tradition of encouraging kindness to animals – the purpose for which it was established – it provides small dog troughs at the base of some of its fountains. Some fountains are given free; in other cases a grant is made towards the cost. At June 1971, the association had provided 2,195 drinking fountains in London and 575 in the provinces and abroad. There were 927 cattle troughs, more or less equally divided between London and elsewhere, and no less than 3,668 dog troughs, of which 2,997 were in London.

Another animal charity which has had to change its aims is the Homes of Rest for Horses, founded in 1886 primarily to look after poor people's horses. The aim today, after approval from the Charity Commissioners, is to assist charities which provide pony riding for the disabled.

The National Trust, largest private landowner in Britain, protects 300 miles of coastline and preserves 200 historic buildings open to the public. At the end of 1971 it had 278,000 members, 75,000 of whom joined during the year, compared with 60,000 in 1970.

Understandably the trust has considerable assets even though no value is placed in the accounts on buildings and land which may never be sold. At the end of 1971 other properties and mortgages were worth £2,357,000, and properties owned and occupied for administrative purposes were worth £469,000. Investments were worth £12,832,000. The total assets of £15,803,000, however, included £10,599,000 in capital endowment funds which may not be spent (only the income used) and £3,733,000 in funds for defined purposes, which may be spent only in certain ways. This left £1,471,000 as the free general reserve of the Trust in that year. Income from property endowments in 1971 came to £2,710,000 (£2,242,000 in 1970). Rents accounted for £865,000 and more than three million visitors to Trust property paid £591,000 in admission fees (£466,000). Membership subscriptions brought in £522,000 (£400,000).

The net cost of maintaining, showing, improving and managing properties not covered by specified funds was £433,000 (£389,000), servicing members £156,000 (£120,000), publicity and recruitment £126,000 (£104,000) and head office administration £169,000 (£152,000). The general fund of the Trust showed a net deficit of £317,000 (£324,000) but this took no account of gifts and legacies and £348,000 (£327,000) was transferred from the central gifts and legacies fund to produce a surplus for the year of £31 (£3). Legacies received during 1971 ranged from £3 to £46,594, to reach a total of £556,208. The general fund also received more than £115,000 in direct gifts. The defined purposes fund started in 1971 at £2,838,000. During the year investment income brought in £100,000, sales of property and leases £12,000, and the market value of investments rose by £523,000. £67,000 was spent on maintaining and showing defined purpose properties, £7,000 on specific appeals, and £188,000 in buying property for preservation.

In 1968 total expenditure by the general and defined purposes funds of the Trust was £2,807,000, in 1969 it was £3,307,000, in 1970 it reached £3,328,000, and in 1971 it was £3,760,000.

The World Wildlife Fund was established with headquarters in Switzerland in 1961. Working closely with the fund are national appeals organizations in many countries. The British National Appeal was the first to be formed, also in 1961, with the Duke of Edinburgh as president. This organization applies at least one-third of the funds it gathers for projects in Britain.

World Wildlife is essentially a fund-raising organization, not a scientific body. The aim is to conserve wild life (defined as 'anything alive and wild') and wild places. They have a 'danger list' of some 1,000 different kinds of animals, birds, fish and insects and some 2,000 species of plants. They are concerned also about population, pollution, pesticides and over-exploitation of the earth's supply of natural resources. And they calculate that world conservation needs up to £5m a year to make headway.

The British National Appeal – like organizations in other countries – raises money in every possible way, but it does not use professional fund-raisers. It rather specializes in the big, glamorous shows and balls but also has hundreds of fund-raising groups throughout the country, a trading company, and a Wildlife Youth Service which, though it is primarily for the education of young people between the ages of 5 and 18, also raises money through its Animals in Danger scheme. Total membership of the British organization in 1971 was 278,000. In that year they also secured 75,000 new members.

Revenue for 1971 was £461,179. Administration, fund-raising and publicity costs came to £102,338. To the balance was added £113,053 carried over from the previous year, providing in all £471,894 for the objects of the fund. Grants made to United Kingdom endowment and capital funds totalled £22,747, to United Kingdom projects, including education, £70,236, and to international projects £118,727. A sum of £260,184 was carried forward and committed to future payments. This meant that the fund spent out of each pound the low figure of 5.4p on administration, but 16.7p on fund-raising and publicity, 6.8p on education, and 71.1p on other projects and purposes.

The type of conservation projects in the United Kingdom supported by the British National Appeal during 1971 included giving grants towards the purchase of wildlife reserves, woods, watercress beds, marshes and similar places. Conducting surveys such as one into the Blue Butterfly, and helping to provide Land Rovers for Conservation Corps workers. International projects ranged the world, including purchases of islands and sanctuaries, surveys of lions in India and research into bear protection in Italy, provision of British staff for Tanzania's National Parks, observing Canadian seal hunts, conservation in Madagascar, and studies of poaching in Peru and Zambia.

21

HELPING THE AGED – 'GENTLEFOLK' OR NOT

By the end of 1974 there probably will be more than nine million people of pensionable age in the United Kingdom – four times as many as at the start of the century – and the population figures suggest that the current net annual rise of 110,000 will continue through the seventies. As elsewhere in the social field, the advances in medicine and consequently longer expectations of life have continued to increase the burden on the Welfare State and on charities.

There are many organizations helping the sick, the handicapped, the mentally ill, the alcoholic and so on, of which the aged form a considerable proportion; in some areas they may be the majority. There are about 70 voluntary organizations to help the aged in various ways, including visiting and combating loneliness, but excluding these, the three main societies specifically formed to tend the elderly are Help the Aged, the Distressed Gentlefolk's Aid Association, and the Royal United Kingdom Beneficient Association. Returning to those comparisons in Chapter 20 between giving to children and animals and adding the total of gifts and legacies received in their 1971 financial years by the three 'aged' charities, we get this picture:

Donated to children	£10,371,000
Donated to animals	£ 3,590,000
Donated to the aged	£ 1,786,000

Certainly, by that standard, it would seem that the British love their animals better than their parents!

In 1971 Help the Aged (seventeenth in the '100 league') had a total income of £1,151,000 (33 per cent up on the previous year). That was all; it had no investments and its assets came to merely £229,000. Yet it is now one of the best-known charities of all *among the young*. Of all charities perhaps it best personifies the work of young people, who do not have much money to give, but do donate themselves and their energies.

Young people 'just curl up' at the very name of the Distressed Gentlefolk's Aid Association – the society itself says so! – and the resources are vastly different. The D.G.A.A. (38 in the league) had gifts and legacies totalling £418,000 (19 per cent down on the previous year) but their 1972 figures, quoted later, were very much better. Assets are more than £3m, but of course this figure includes the value of homes they run.

The Royal United Kingdom Beneficient Association, with a somewhat more acceptable, if no less Victorian, name than the D.G.A.A., had gifts and legacies of £217,000 in 1971 (52 per cent of the previous year). Assets of nearly £7.5m again included residential homes.

Help the Aged is primarily, but by no means entirely, concerned in Britain with housing the elderly. The statistics of old age in this country today are depressing. Sixty thousand people, mostly elderly, die each year of cold-associated illnesses; 350,000 old people have neither kitchen, inside lavatory, or use of a bathroom; 1.2m lack two of these amenities; 1.5m people over 65 live in complete isolation – perhaps one of the most disturbing facts of all and a reason why Help the Aged does not regard poverty as an essential criterion for help: loneliness can be at least as important. Sometimes loneliness can be fatal. During the general election of February, 1974, canvassers in Peterborough, Lincolnshire, found two old age pensioners dead on successive days. Both were elderly women who had been living alone. They had been dead for some days. In one case the home had to be broken open to reach the woman. And on a third day canvassers in the same city found an old woman lying on the floor, unable to move or call for assistance. She too lived entirely alone.

The trouble about this kind of thing is that little of it is *seen* as a rule; it is hidden behind walls, walls of brick and of pride, and many of the victims never even go out to tell anyone about their condition. While screening applicants for assistance, Help the Aged recorded just some of the terrible conditions they found:

"We saw people living in rooms with mildew on the walls, green mould on the windows. We saw holes in the floor, we saw rooms with damp, almost sodden bedding. There were others whose rooms were lice-ridden, with gas-lighting. There were people who *never* had a visitor . . ." They found a former nurse living in a damp basement, infested with lice, cockroaches, worms and rats. The only heating was an oil stove, and it cost 30p to have a bath. The lavatory was outside and everyone in the house had to go through her room to use it."

Many of the people assisted by Help the Aged were once well-off – 'distressed gentlefolk' indeed. Men can lose their livelihoods overnight, women can be widowed in an instant. Poverty, ill-health, loneliness and bad housing are of course inter-related. Old people on minimal incomes can rarely get single rooms; they have to move into the worst accommodation in the land. It is calculated that more than a million old people would be in rooms of their own if they could be found – 42 per cent of all old people live with their children and families, often none-too-happily. One in ten of the people crowding Britain's geriatric wards could be moved out . . . if there was anywhere for them to go. Most of the elderly in residential homes could live independently, again if there was anywhere for them to go.

Here are just four extracts from old people's letters of despair, quoted in Help the Aged's report on housing conditions, '*Granny Come Home*':

> " 'Sundays I usually have an Oxo and bread for dinner – and of course at Christmas I'm lucky if I can afford a pork chop.'
>
> 'When I have nothing I just fall asleep and forget everything.'
>
> 'The coat I am wearing my daughter gave me 25 years ago.'
>
> 'I pray at night that God will take me.' "

What, then, does Help the Aged do and how did it come into existence?

In 1953 a group of British businessmen decided to bring their joint experience into fund-raising and established 'Voluntary Christian Causes' to raise money for elderly refugees, predominantly abroad. In 1960 'Voluntary and Christian Service' was formed, again largely to help old people overseas, but in 1964 it was decided to concentrate on old people in Britain through Help the Aged, now the biggest arm of V.C.S. Help the Aged works from almost impossibly over-crowded offices in an unimpressive building in Denman Street, off Piccadilly. The small rooms are jammed, mostly with young people, quite a proportion of whom are working for less than what they would get in the open labour market. Even though it may be true that the young can afford to do this – for a time – there is undoubtedly a remarkable aura of idealism and dedication in Denman Street.

Help the Aged runs what is now one of the biggest housing

associations in the country, providing sheltered homes for elderly people of limited means who – given some support – are able to look after themselves. These people are selected from local authorities' lists, from names put forward by the National Old People's Welfare Council and other welfare bodies, and from those who apply directly to the society. They began by adapting existing homes but today a typical sheltered housing scheme consists of 24 to 36 purpose-built self-contained flats, together with common rooms and resident warden's accommodation. The flats are let at an economic rent and they are largely unfurnished so that tenants may have their own possessions around them, if they have any. The flats are centrally heated and the resident warden, who is linked to all flats by two-way inter-com, is there to provide an element of background care and help where necessary.

The first such scheme was completed only in 1969 but by the end of December, 1971, Help the Aged had £13,601,000 worth of housing in hand, helped by 100 per cent local authority mortgages. By now the figure is more than £17m. Occupied flats in 1971 totalled 500, with 2,764 under construction. The society points out that a donation of £1 to Help the Aged can be turned into £25 worth of flat. A project for 38 flats, for example, could be financed in 1971 for an outlay of £5,000 from Help the Aged, with £150,000 capital costs met by the local authority, repayable over 60 years at subsidized interest rates. Rentals charged to tenants are subsidized if necessary by the Government. But Help the Aged has to pay for the enormous amount of work involved in finding housing sites and carrying out lengthy negotiations, and each project incurs many costs not met by the local authority, such as furniture and curtains for spare guest rooms where provided, and the furnishing of the common rooms, carpets, gardening, laundry and cleaning equipment. There are now Help the Aged flats all over the country. And apart from that reassuring two-way communication system linked to every bedroom, the old people are lonely no longer; indeed a considerable social life invariably builds up around each unit, with coach outings, coffee mornings, bingo, whist drives, and so on. There is often a total transformation in the physical and mental health of the inhabitants. As Help the Aged puts it "Happiness in old age in total contrast to the misery we have described . . . it's a thrilling story."

Backing up its housing activities, Help the Aged issues reports on the condition of the elderly, and a typical one was

'Telephones for the Aged – a Matter of Life or Death', issued in 1972. This showed up the inability of local authorities to assist because of the rules laid down for the provision of telephones, though in many cases people are far from help of any kind in emergency. For example, one woman had frequently to walk a quarter of a mile in the middle of the night to a farmer's telephone to summon the doctor for her husband, who was subject to recurrent heart trouble. The report showed that in one year in a group supplied with telephones through the Duchess of Norfolk's Telephones for the Aged Appeal, run by Help the Aged, there were exactly half the number of deaths as in a control group without telephones.

To carry out its work Help the Aged raises money through Christmas cards, nearly 50 gift shops, general appeals, and appeals for specific causes, such as a disaster abroad. Children and young people play a big role, though there are plenty of pensioners who send money, and so does Big Business. Says the organization:

> The response from young people to our work is incredible. There is great feeling for the old among the young. The young do not take an attitude about the Welfare State, unlike the middle-aged they do not expect it to do everything. The young regard it as their job to give a lead to the Welfare State. The young engage in all sorts of activities, they stage swims, walks, go digging gardens. There are hundreds of school groups, and one young people's group in Enfield raised enough for a complete housing scheme in their area. The young are of course much more forceful in their approach, they don't recognize obstacles . . . they charge ahead – successfully!

The society has paid youth organizers throughout the country to visit schools and clubs, but has no flag days, pays no commission to anyone. As with other charities, they have changed their advertising approach. Once it was along the lines 'Old age can't be helped but the loneliness and misery can'. Now advertisements emphasize more what can be done for the old, helping them to live life to the full.

Help the Aged's £1,151,169 of revenue in 1971 included £808,547 from appeals and gifts in kind, £54,985 in convenanted gifts and legacies – as a young organization legacies are still low – £238,893 from specific appeals and £49,744 from the gift shops. Appeal expenses reached £166,648 and administration expenses £42,907. Distribution during the year came to £905,644 and £214,128 was carried forward to 1972. Of the distribution figure, £214,369 was spent in Britain and £691,275 abroad, where the organization sends grants for food, medicines and shelter to established and trusted bodies in different countries, such as the Salvation Army, Mother Teresa's Missionaries of Charity, Caritas, Protestant missionaries and so on. During the year more than a million items of clothing were shipped, (collected by opening church halls all over Britain for two or three-day appeals) and, of course, blankets, for which there is an insatiable call. The clothing went to refugees in the Middle East, Hong Kong, Cambodia, Africa, and to welfare bodies dealing with poverty in places like Nairobi, Madras, Bombay and Calcutta. Scores of overseas organizations received funds to provide a quarter of a million Christmas meals for destitute old people, with subscribers in Britain sponsoring the meals at 20p a time. £10,000 and 200 bales of clothing were sent to Bangladesh. Help the Aged also contributes to six eye hospitals overseas, including one at Allahabad, where the lone Hindu doctor, Dr J.C. Bass, also goes out to the villages around, sets up a makeshift operating unit, and carries out delicate cataract operations on the aged, under local anaesthetic. Comments Help the Aged: "When you think that £75 will cover the cost of a day's cataract operations that restore sight to 30 people, it would be hard to think of a happier use of money." Indeed.

The Distressed Gentlefolk's Aid Association has for quite a time considered changing that name that is so off-putting to the young, though it is believed to attract the middle-aged Says the organization: "Should the word 'gentlefolk' be incarcerated with the Victorians? It's a moot point, but nevertheless there are people who through hereditary background have been taught that they must be independent and provide for their own future; they have a pride in their ability to remain self-sufficient. Among them are many who, no matter how hard they try, cannot meet the rising cost of living and the modern way of life." And the D.G.A.A. will add, frankly, that to alter the name would – on the experience of other charities – probably result in a drastic fall in income for five years or so, until people got accustomed to the change.

At any given time the D.G.A.A. will have some 1,500 beneficiaries, falling into three main groups: (1) the majority, elderly men and women living in their own homes, with reduced incomes, who are helped to enjoy a reasonably comfortable and happy life; (2) ill and infirm people in need of care and attention who, if they cannot be taken into one of D.G.A.A.'s own homes, are helped with fees for other homes; and (3) the younger incapacitated people and mothers with young families who find themselves wholly responsible for keeping the home going and looking after the children. Here help is given to maintain the home while the children are launched on a career and also to finance a family holiday.

That feeling of independence, that pride that the D.G.A.A. refers to, in itself creates part of the need. Again and again cases come up of people who could *get by* – if they depended on their children or continued living with them. There is not among such people that great fear of 'homes' and institutions found elsewhere, possibly because many have seen much of the work done in such places during their own activities in helping charity in one way or another. They are anxious to take the burden off their children . . . if they can go anywhere else that they can afford. For such people the D.G.A.A. has residential homes at Woodbridge, Suffolk, and Eastbourne, Sussex, as well as 17 flatlets in a converted private school in Tunbridge Wells, Kent, paid for by the Worshipful Company of Innholders. There are residential and nursing homes at Harrogate, Yorkshire, and Exeter, Devon, and nursing homes at Laverstock, Kent, Merlewood, Surrey, Wychbold, Worcestershire, Wallingford, Berkshire, and at Vicarage Gate House in London's Kensington, which is also the headquarters of the association.

To maintain all these establishments and run the organization, the D.G.A.A. had in 1971/72 a weekly average of 378 employees, costing a total of £368,657, about £32,000 up on the previous year. Expenditure on homes took £476,450, including part of the wages and salary figure, and the cost of helping individual cases with regular allowances (usually allocated on a long-term basis to provide a feeling of security), food, clothing and fuel, came to £172,407. The D.G.A.A. has more than 70 beneficiaries living abroad and a typical example is that of a young man, Timothy, who had been an orphan from his early years, unable to work through constant bad health, and who lived with his grandmother in Italy on a joint income of £4.62 a week. Given a regular allowance, Timothy and grandmother were re-housed and enabled to live free from anxiety.

During the year fees from patients and sundry receipts brought in £142,983, subscriptions and donations of all kinds, including allocations from Trusts and City Livery

Companies, came to £116,452, and interest and dividends on more than £2.8m of investments to £184,426. There was an excess of expenditure over general income of £260,209 but in that year – its 75th anniversary – the D.G.A.A. received no less than £533,536 in legacies and special gifts, which left a surplus for general funds of £273,326. Total expenditure for the year reached £720,523, of which administration accounted for only £45,663.

Probably no charity has so many lords and ladies among its supporters as the D.G.A.A. – and its lists of council and committees read like extracts from *Debrett*. In 1972 the council of management showed 14 titles and the appeals committee seven more. Two of the permanent executive staff are baronets, the patron is the Queen Mother and the president the Duchess of Kent.

This is very much reflected in the association's fund-raising methods and the people who conduct them. During the year the Queen Mother attended a concert given by Joseph Cooper at St James's Palace to mark the 75th anniversary, while the Duchess of Kent attended a 'Fashion Spectacular' staged by Marks & Spencer at – no less – the Banqueting Hall, Whitehall. But it is when one looks at the massive county organization and the work done here that the rarified flavour of the D.G.A.A. is most apparent. From the lists of money raised during the year here are some random examples: Bedfordshire garden party £204; Buckinghamshire bridge morning £100, bring-and-buy sale £309, fête £530; cake stall at Cardigan market £26.63; Chelsea bridge party £300; Devon Christmas bazaar £715; buffet lunch and recital at a helper's home £300; Gloucestershire plant sale £651, fashion show £652; Hampshire fashion show £635; Kent autumn fair £970; Oxfordshire fête £3,614; Regency ball at Bath £770; Marks & Spencer dress show at Castle Howard, Yorkshire £1,112; and a 'Going for a Song' evening, held in a private home and with experts from both Sothebys and Spinks helping £369.

Most such events were staged in private homes and gardens and even in London the tradition continues. £3,300 was made by a flower ball, using a rectory garden, organized by the Kensington and Chelsea committee of the association. £122 came from 'Tea in a Knightsbridge garden', while a spring luncheon at the Vicarage Gate headquarters raised £526. The Westminister committee got £300 from a St Patrick's Day lunch, Tombola brought in £876, and 'Champagne at the Ritz' with a Louis Feraud fashion show contributed £650.

Few if anybody can beat the D.G.A.A. at this sort of thing! Obviously most of the support came from the middle-aged and relatively well-off, but what about the young people? Says the association: "The youngsters regard our name as snobbish but they help . . . when told to do so! They'll sell tickets for example. The real initiative comes from the older people." Understandably, the D.G.A.A. does not need to use fund-raisers or professional organizers of any kind. Incidentally, among the D.G.A.A.'s income which may only be applied for specific purposes is the Helvetia Trust, consisting of £100 bequeathed by a Scotsman for a Scottish widow annually to have a holiday in Mentone. The trust was named Helvetia because the Scotsman had owned a ship of the name.

The D.G.A.A. works very closely with R.U.K.B.A., the Royal United Kingdom Beneficient Association, co-ordinating assistance in many cases and avoiding overlapping so far as possible, though there are occasions when both may agree to help the same person.

While there are not quite as many titles associated with R.U.K.B.A., of which the Queen Mother is also patron, the other patrons, vice-presidents and committee members still constitute an impressive list of names from the peerage, the churches, and the upper echelons of the armed forces. Founded in 1863 and with a Royal Charter dating from 1911, the primary object of the association is to grant annuities without regard to sex or religious denomination to gentlefolk – again! – in very strained circumstances, resident in the British Isles, who are free from any unsoundness of mind and being over 40 years of age are, because of bodily infirmity, unable to earn their own livelihood. The original annuity granted in 1864 was £15, but by 1971/72 it had been raised to £156, with an income limit of £600 for a single person and £1,100 for married couples. The basic idea is to provide permanent annuities to help beneficiaries to live their own independent lives in their own homes for as long as possible. In addition, those still in need may get help from a relief fund and a clothing department.

But by 1949 it had become apparent that there was a great need for residential homes for old people and R.U.K.B.A. was granted powers to provide homes and to co-operate with other charitable organizations in this field. R.U.K.B.A. helps to maintain people in homes for the infirm (which include 145 nursing care places), homes for the aged, 145 places, and in nursing homes, 66 places. In addition, the association has two homes of its own, catering for more than 120 people. At the end of 1971 R.U.K.B.A. had 4,291 annuitants on its books, an increase of 532 on the previous year, the largest rise in the history of the association to date, and bringing the number since foundation to nearly 19,000. During the year expenditure on relief grants went up by some £4,200, reflecting increased need at a time of rapid inflation.

Through about 750 honorary workers in nearly 600 auxiliary branches throughout the country, R.U.K.B.A. raised money in most of the usual ways. Of the total receipts in 1971 of £828,213, legacies provided £205,817, and about £516,000 came from rents and investments. Aggregate expenditure was £711,950, of which £62,000 was the net cost of the two R.U.K.B.A. homes, administration expenses were £93,810, and costs of general relief work, staff salaries, and expenses 'in the field' were £18,222. In the year annuities accounted for £411,396, relief grants and gifts £50,159, and grants-in-aid for maintenance in other homes £51,140. The amount distributed in all forms came to £576,305, plus 2,334 parcels of clothing and provisions, worth £11,720, sent to beneficiaries. There was an excess of receipts over payments on the income account for the year of £27,646.

Though R.U.K.B.A. had total funds at the end of the year of £7,422,352, no less than £5,123,780 represented trust funds, of which only the income could be used. The balance was made up of the value of the homes and the funds required for the payment of life annuities; each life annuity calls for a capital sum of about £1,000 to be placed in reserve.

What sort of people does R.U.K.B.A. help within its charter to 'support gentlefolk in need'? There is the daughter of a Church of England missionary who was a nursing sister until her marriage in 1909 to a textile merchant. He died in 1937 and her only income was ten pounds *a year* until, at the age of 90, she was taken into a R.U.K.B.A. residential home. There is the man who served in the Merchant Navy from 1907 to 1931 (except for World War I service with the Royal Navy) and reached the rank of Chief Officer, when he had to retire through ill-health. Nonetheless he served again in World War II, reaching the rank of Captain R.N.R. After the war he went into business but lost most of his capital. Housebound with illness, he and his wife, both R.U.K.B.A. annuitants, were also provided with a bungalow.

The daughter of a well-known actor, she was trained in

horticulture and agriculture and, nearing 70, she still earns a few pounds in the summer as a part-time gardener. Her only other income was a retirement pension and £60 a year from her brother, but now, she has a R.U.K.B.A. annuity.

A Methodist Minister for 41 years, whose wife died in 1969. He is 85, but looks after his invalid daughter – helped by the association.

Daughter of a naval officer, her marriage to a famous racing motorist was dissolved. She was supported by her son until he was killed. Until the association came to her aid, her only income was her supplementary pension and an annuity of £16.

Son of a South African broker and himself a river transport agent in Zambia, he came to England in 1954, invented and manufactured a well-known gardening tool. The business failed for lack of capital and his only income, at the age of 80, was a charitable grant of £50 a year. Both he and his wife, a former school teacher, became annuitants.

A last example: someone who has experienced tragedy to the full but is now at least more secure with R.U.K.B.A. help. Her husband, manager of an overseas bank, was killed while a Japanese prisoner-of-war, her R.A.F. pilot son died during the Battle of Britain, her daughter died at sea when her ship was torpedoed. She had very slight resources but even these were reduced by illness and she had to have the toes of her right foot amputated.

22

BEER AND BENEVOLENCE

Once sacrosanct so far as criticism was concerned, almost revered among charities, the Royal British Legion is by no means so highly regarded everywhere today. This is rather unfair, though to a large extent it is its own fault. It is often assailed as being little more than a huge social society, a collection of clubs and halls for bibulous war veterans. The very active social side, and what some see as a failure to put over its own image properly, cloud the picture. They do indeed lower the beer in those clubs, but they undertake a tremendous amount of benevolent work as well.

The 1971 golden jubilee year report on the Legion records no less than 17,582 cases of various kinds dealt with by headquarters, 3,824 more by area organizations, and 'thousands' of others handled by about 4,300 local committees in England and Wales, and Northern and Southern Ireland.

The British Legion was formed in 1921 by bringing together four national organizations of ex-servicemen which had been formed after World War I. The 'Royal' prefix was granted for the golden jubilee. The Legion puts its aims in this order: (1) to perpetuate the memory of those who died in the service of their country, (2) to educate public opinion to the view that the maintenance of the disabled and the welfare of ex-servicemen, women and dependants are national duties, (3) to press the claims of ex-servicemen for employment and to secure not less than the recognized standard rates of wages in accordance with their ability, (4) to assist ex-servicemen and women and the widows, children and dependants of those who have served, in matters relating to pensions, allowances, grants and war gratuities, (5) to raise co-ordinated funds for the purpose of assisting ex-servicemen and their dependants, and (6) to assist serving men in connection with their return to civil life and to promote the interests of their dependants while they are serving.

Ordinary membership of the Legion is open to ex-servicemen and women who have served at least seven days with the Colours and received seven days' pay (*except conscientous objectors*): men and women of the Merchant Marine who have served afloat during hostilities outside territorial waters; men and women of the St John Ambulance Association, the British Red Cross Society and the St Andrew's Ambulance Association, provided they have served with the forces of the Crown; and any British or naturalized British subject who has served at least seven days during hostilities with the forces of an allied nation and has received seven days' pay.

And, rare in the charity field, the Legion makes only one boast: "The machinery of the Legion is entirely democratic, enabling as it does every individual member to have a voice in its affairs and to obtain by a democratic vote of the members of the Legion the highest positions in the organization." The structure is simple. Each member of the Legion must belong to a branch. Eleven areas nominate representatives to the national executive council and nominees are elected by the annual conference. There is also a women's section, which widows and dependants of ex-servicemen may also join.

In 1971 membership was about 750,000, of which about 160,000 were in the women's section. Although about 27,000 members are lost annually through death and other causes, there was a net increase of 42,000 members on the previous year. However, there are between four and five million ex-servicemen and women in Britain and Ireland who remain outside the Legion. The men had 4,283 branches – 58 of them overseas – and the women 2,764 self-supporting branches, of which five were overseas. There were in addition 1,028 affiliated clubs and the Legion is also trustee for 129 United Services clubs. The 4,300 local committees, totalling at least 50,000 voluntary social workers, help to administer the benevolent fund. It is certainly a vast organization.

At 30 September 1971 the Legion had assets of £3,229,448, of which £1,792,852 represented investments recorded at cost. Income of the benevolent fund for the year was £1,741,502, of which the 1970 Poppy Appeal brought in £1,201,839 – compared with £106,000 in 1921 – and the sale of wreaths £138,170. General donations came only to £19,824. Against this total of £1,359,833, the cost of producing 27.4m poppies was

£150,395. The benevolent fund spent £1,494,667 during the year, including £927,053 in grants and the net maintenance cost of homes, £74,482 on appeals and administration, more than £40,000 on publicity and advertising, and a massive £233,572 on 'cost of service'. There was therefore a deficit on the benevolent account of £134,833, but the fund was kept in balance by various sums, including the £67,371 received in legacies in the year, to show a surplus of £4,635. On the Legion's general account, affiliation fees and other charges paid by branches realized £160,468. But what is recorded as 'administration and special functions' took £163,411 and publicity and advertising a further £18,574. All in all, there was a deficit on this account of £22,776, met by donations, interest and dividends, and sundry other incomes, aggregating £62,102, to show a surplus for the year of £39,326.

Out of the £927,053 spent on grants, £550,544 went for rehabilitation and the relief of distress, £122,958 on country and rest homes, £23,346 to various Legion schemes, including trading companies, £3,241 on visits to war graves, £30,000 to the poppy factory, and £110,000 to the Officers' Benevolent Department. A breakdown of the relief expenditure provides a good picture of the work done by the Legion. Local committees spent £185,634 on temporary and immediate needs, area offices spent £39,634 where further, protracted help was necessary, £219,504 went on 8,890 monthly allowances to incapacitated ex-servicemen and women and to widows (widows were more than half of the total here). Headquarters spent £77,364 on cases such as removals, surgical appliances, burying indigent ex-servicemen, avoiding the break-up of family life, preventing evictions, and grants for distress. Seaside holidays were provided for 176 severely disabled ex-servicemen, of whom 109 were accompanied by wives or relatives, and to six disabled ex-servicewomen. No less than 15,797 patients were visited in 515 establishments and £17,604 was spent by headquarters on comforts and outings for them.

Apart from this sort of activity, the Legion has always devoted considerable attention to housing, and £2.3m had been lent by the Legion and co-operating funds by 1971 to help house purchase, of which £2.2m had been repaid. The scheme is entirely self-sufficient. Loans go mostly to ex-regulars who have not completed enough service to qualify them for resettlement grants. The difficult type of case is that of the man who is invalided and must move his family from married quarters. The Legion's own Housing Association built 1,000 flatlets for the needy, elderly and widows in various parts of the country between 1966 and 1971 and 2,000 more were under construction or at advanced planning stage. Purpose-built, the flatlets are usually in units of about 40 and the provision of this accommodation is of course freeing homes sorely needed by younger people.

Different from any other village in the United Kingdom is Preston Hall and its British Legion village near Maidstone, Kent. Since 1925 the Legion has built up here the largest organization in the world for the treatment, training and rehabilitation of ex-servicemen and women, originally suffering from tuberculosis but, with the lower incidence of T.B. today, mainly from other illnesses, including a variety of chest, heart and physically disabled cases and some with slight mental disturbances. A hospital with more than 500 beds, the nurses' home and the manor of Preston Hall itself are operated today under the National Health Service but the workshops, hotels, flats, and 109 houses forming the village are owned by the Legion. In 1971 no less than £95,000 was paid out in wages and salaries to workers in the village, where 150 ex-servicemen or their dependants were employed. There were 110 places in hostels for disabled men undergoing rehabilitation or training.

The work done here covers quite a considerable range. One department makes road signs for local authorities, British Rail and others. Another turns out different kinds of fencing and gates, others produce garden sheds, boxes and export packing cases as well as many other timber components. The fancy goods department sends a quarter of its light woodwork to the Legion women's section branches, a quarter to shops, and the balance is sub-contracted to large manufacturers. They produce things like expanding clothes airers, stools, deck chairs, and wooden plant stands, but also Christmas cards and toilet soap. The printing department is one of the best-equipped of its kind in the area and turns out general commercial work as well as Legion publications.

There is no doubt that if Preston Hall were run on strictly commercial lines it could make substantial profits but the needs of the disabled take priority – that is what it is all about – and the 1971 deficit was £31,562, though about three-quarters of the £27,463 trading loss was

recoverable from the Government
the balance was met by central
£2,000 worth of goods were exp
Preston Hall company's 1971 ass
It was in 1929 that the Le
most successful ventures, the T
During 1970/71 the school tu
and there were another 12
brought the total since th
disabled or ex-regular servic
drivers.
Outside the Government,
employer of the disabled, w
any given time. One of t
'Attendants Company'. T
women – ex-service and o
security wardens, commi
parking areas. At 30
employed 854 men an
full-time, 235 part-tim
were disabled people a
the Legion. Wages and
and unlike other
welcomed the fact t
£102,124 in the yea
worthwhile employm
had a net operating
than 20 per cent
make £10,656 in
cost of a new reha
towards the life
National Lifeboa
The Legion rai
named 'The Ro
After dona
company had
£302,046.
The Legion
sells articles
the year rise
of £773. As
With ass
factory a
poppies, 1
3,420 spe

ex-se
home
56,48
from
£27,15
At I
Factory
wools,
disabled
financial
but mad
£16,037
During
admitted
The net
£58,036
Navy Bene
Fund. It t
residential
local autho
Then the
headquarter
opened and
1,168 succes
and allowan
and lump s
those cases a
1939 onward
Legion had s
payments for
previously rej
specialists and
appeal tribunal
of appeals and
the tribunals.
In January
Cambridge Univ
the rag week
because they fe
from students w
as a 'war charity'
in at once to
Telegraph from S
"Do those maime
go hungry in Asia

For some years an Ulster Unionist M.P. at Westminster, Sir Knox probably had Northern Ireland very much in mind, even though there is, officially, no 'war' there. The 1971 Legion report tells a little of the story:

> In expressing its appreciation of the voluntary work undertaken by those who give unstintingly of their time and services as members of local Service Committees, an especial tribute is due to the men and women who continue to work under the difficult and sometimes dangerous conditions which prevail in Northern Ireland. With many ex-Service families living in the troubled areas in Belfast, Londonderry and elsewhere, there have been numerous calls upon the Legion for financial aid. Generally cash grants have been made for the purchase of clothing and other necessities. The Royal British Legion itself has not escaped the attention of the terrorists. Several branch and club premises have been damaged by bombs, both in the North and in the Irish Republic. In Dublin the area office was severely damaged and had to be vacated. The sympathy and admiration of the whole Legion goes out to our comrades in Northern and Southern Ireland who are carrying on the true spirit of comradeship without regard to religious or political convictions.

Some little time later the Legion disclosed that Northern Ireland was contributing more money per head of population to the Legion than any other part of the United Kingdom.

23

CARING TILL DEATH

Those charity officials who held that Dr Barnardo's was the most efficient of all voluntary organizations almost invariably added something like, "But then, there is of course the Cheshire Foundation, a wonderful organization . . . and quite unique."

The Cheshire Foundation Homes for the Sick *is* a remarkable charity because, in one sense, of its very lack of organization and centralization, and because once somebody enters one of their homes he or she is virtually there for life, cared for until death.

Started in 1948, more or less by accident, the Cheshire Foundation has today 62 homes, hostels and special block of flats, for men, women and children in the United Kingdom, with more than 2,000 residents, and a further 66 establishments stretching across the world, with 1,300 more residents.

Group Captain Leonard Cheshire is world famous. In RAF Bomber Command he won the Victoria Cross, the Distinguished Service Order with two bars, and the Distinguished Flying Cross and he was an official British observer when the second atomic bomb was dropped on Nagasaki in 1945. When he retired from the R.A.F. as soon as peace was declared he wanted to do something to make peace a reality and started a co-operative community scheme for ex-servicemen, but it failed. He was winding up this abortive project in May, 1948 and trying to get rid of the large, empty house, Le Court, near Liss in Hampshire, where he had tried to organize his settlement, when he was told that one of the former members of the settlement, a man of 75, was dying in hospital of cancer and had nowhere else to go. Cheshire hunted for some place where the man could end his days in peace but eventually took him into Le Court and nursed him till he died. Personally quite unable to resist any appeal, Cheshire then took in others – with no idea at all where the money was to come

case is that of the man who is invalided and must move his family from married quarters. The Legion's own Housing Association built 1,000 flatlets for the needy, elderly and widows in various parts of the country between 1966 and 1971 and 2,000 more were under construction or at advanced planning stage. Purpose-built, the flatlets are usually in units of about 40 and the provision of this accommodation is of course freeing homes sorely needed by younger people.

Different from any other village in the United Kingdom is Preston Hall and its British Legion village near Maidstone, Kent. Since 1925 the Legion has built up here the largest organization in the world for the treatment, training and rehabilitation of ex-servicemen and women, originally suffering from tuberculosis but, with the lower incidence of T.B. today, mainly from other illnesses, including a variety of chest, heart and physically disabled cases and some with slight mental disturbances. A hospital with more than 500 beds, the nurses' home and the manor of Preston Hall itself are operated today under the National Health Service but the workshops, hotels, flats, and 109 houses forming the village are owned by the Legion. In 1971 no less than £95,000 was paid out in wages and salaries to workers in the village, where 150 ex-servicemen or their dependants were employed. There were 110 places in hostels for disabled men undergoing rehabilitation or training.

The work done here covers quite a considerable range. One department makes road signs for local authorities, British Rail and others. Another turns out different kinds of fencing and gates, others produce garden sheds, boxes and export packing cases as well as many other timber components. The fancy goods department sends a quarter of its light woodwork to the Legion women's section branches, a quarter to shops, and the balance is sub-contracted to large manufacturers. They produce things like expanding clothes airers, stools, deck chairs, and wooden plant stands, but also Christmas cards and toilet soap. The printing department is one of the best-equipped of its kind in the area and turns out general commercial work as well as Legion publications.

There is no doubt that if Preston Hall were run on strictly commercial lines it could make substantial profits but the needs of the disabled take priority – that is what it is all about – and the 1971 deficit was £31,562, though about three-quarters of the £27,463 trading loss was

£150,395. The benevolent fund spent £1,494,667 during the year, including £927,053 in grants and the net maintenance cost of homes, £74,482 on appeals and administration, more than £40,000 on publicity and advertising, and a massive £233,572 on 'cost of service'. There was therefore a deficit on the benevolent account of £134,833, but the fund was kept in balance by various sums, including the £67,371 received in legacies in the year, to show a surplus of £4,635. On the Legion's general account, affiliation fees and other charges paid by branches realized £160,468. But what is recorded as 'administration and special functions' took £163,411 and publicity and advertising a further £18,574. All in all, there was a deficit on this account of £22,776, met by donations, interest and dividends, and sundry other incomes, aggregating £62,102, to show a surplus for the year of £39,326.

Out of the £927,053 spent on grants, £550,544 went for rehabilitation and the relief of distress, £122,958 on country and rest homes, £23,346 to various Legion schemes, including trading companies, £3,241 on visits to war graves, £30,000 to the poppy factory, and £110,000 to the Officers' Benevolent Department. A breakdown of the relief expenditure provides a good picture of the work done by the Legion. Local committees spent £185,634 on temporary and immediate needs, area offices spent £39,634 where further, protracted help was necessary, £219,504 went on 8,890 monthly allowances to incapacitated ex-servicemen and women and to widows (widows were more than half of the total here). Headquarters spent £77,364 on cases such as removals, surgical appliances, burying indigent ex-servicemen, avoiding the break-up of family life, preventing evictions, and grants for distress. Seaside holidays were provided for 176 severely disabled ex-servicemen, of whom 109 were accompanied by wives or relatives, and to six disabled ex-servicewomen. No less than 15,797 patients were visited in 515 establishments and £17,604 was spent by headquarters on comforts and outings for them.

Apart from this sort of activity, the Legion has always devoted considerable attention to housing, and £2.3m had been lent by the Legion and co-operating funds by 1971 to help house purchase, of which £2.2m had been repaid. The scheme is entirely self-sufficient. Loans go mostly to ex-regulars who have not completed enough service to qualify them for resettlement grants. The difficult type of

recoverable from the Government and local authorities and the balance was met by central Legion funds. Just over £2,000 worth of goods were exported during the year. The Preston Hall company's 1971 assets were put at £588,870.

It was in 1929 that the Legion established one of its most successful ventures, the Taxi Drivers Training School. During 1970/71 the school turned out 138 trained drivers and there were another 124 under instruction. That brought the total since the scheme started to 4,295 disabled or ex-regular servicemen trained as London taxi drivers.

Outside the Government, the Legion is Britain's largest employer of the disabled, with about 1,500 on the rolls at any given time. One of the organizations is the Legion's 'Attendants Company'. This provides disabled men and women – ex-service and otherwise – as car park attendants, security wardens, commissionaires, and guards at security parking areas. At 30 September 1971 the company employed 854 men and 18 women, of whom 477 were full-time, 235 part-time, and 160 'casual'. Well over half were disabled people and 498 were ordinary members of the Legion. Wages and salaries for the year cost £535,520, and unlike other employers, the Legion positively welcomed the fact that wages and salaries had risen by £102,124 in the year, for it is the constant aim to provide worthwhile employment at the 'going rates'. The company had a net operating turnover of £661,496, which was more than 20 per cent up on the previous year. It was able to make £10,656 in donations, including £3,000 towards the cost of a new rehabilitation unit at Preston Hall and £3,000 towards the lifeboat which was bought for the Royal National Lifeboat Institute to celebrate the Legion's jubilee. The Legion raised £51,141 for this lifeboat, which was named 'The Royal British Legion Jubilee'.

After donations and capital costs the Attendants company had a trading surplus of £11,999 and assets of £302,046.

The Legion's 'Disabled Men's Industries Limited', which sells articles made by disabled ex-servicemen, saw sales for the year rise by £4,465 to £50,971 and return a net profit of £773. Assets were £31,240.

With assets of £266,055, the Legion's famous poppy factory at Richmond, Surrey, produced 27,414,000 poppies, 180,000 remembrance crosses, 50,651 wreaths and 3,420 special wreaths in the year. Employing 150 disabled ex-servicemen at the factory and 79 more in their own homes, the unit also delivered 1,271,500 car stickers, 56,487 rosettes and 53,601 lapel badges, including orders from New York and Japan. Trading profit for the year was £27,150, compared with £8,252 the previous year.

At Llanwrtyd Wells, Breconshire, the Legion's Cambrian Factory Ltd produces quality Welsh tweeds, knitting wools, scarves, travelling rugs and so on, all made by the disabled. With assets of £74,503 at the end of the 1970/71 financial year, the company sold £51,671 worth of goods but made a net loss of £11,828, compared with a loss of £16,037 the previous year.

During the 1971 financial year 3,019 patients were admitted to the Legion's four convalescent and rest homes. The net cost of running the homes rose by £2,508 to £58,036 but the Legion was helped here by the Royal Navy Benevolent Fund and the Royal Air Force Benevolent Fund. It took the record figure of £226,099 to run the five residential country homes, a rise of more than £23,000, but local authority help reduced the increase to about £7,000.

Then there is the enormous amount of work handled by headquarters. In the year, 4,760 new pension cases were opened and, in all, 10,000 such cases were dealt with and 1,168 successes recorded. The annual value of the pensions and allowances thus secured was £148,132 and cash arrears and lump settlements came to £118,574. Forty-four of those cases arose from World War I and the remainder from 1939 onwards. From 1945 to 30 September 1971 the Legion had secured almost £4m in arrears and lump-sum payments for appellants. In presenting claims that had been previously rejected, the Legion consulted 102 medical specialists and represented more than 2,000 claimants at appeal tribunals. The Legion was successful in 37 per cent of appeals and had 663 more successes without reference to the tribunals.

In January 1973, the Press reported the decision of Cambridge University students not to make a grant from the rag week collection to the Legion's poppy appeal because they felt they would thereby gain more support from students who were anti-war and regarded the Legion as a 'war charity'. Among the disgusted letters that flowed in at once to the newspapers was one in the *Daily Telegraph* from Sir Knox Cunningham Q.C., who asked: "Do those maimed in war need help less than others who go hungry in Asia or are addicted to drugs in England? . . ."

from. Arrangements at Le Court in the early days were makeshift to say the least but they were better than hospital geriatric wards for example and, above all, it was a real 'home', in the fullest possible sense of the word. Le Court was the first and for two years the only Cheshire Home; today it has been replaced by a large modern building that is a model of its kind in the country.

In 1950 Cheshire started a second home in the abandoned station headquarters of an old R.A.F. airfield in Cornwall. Then the concept snowballed to become the astonishing organization it is now, with homes or hostels of one kind or another throughout the United Kingdom and Eire, in Canada, Ceylon, Chile, Ethiopia, Hong Kong, India, Israel, Kenya, Malaysia, Mauritius, Morocco, Nigeria, Papua and New Guinea, the Philippines, Portugal, Sierre Leone, Singapore, South Africa, Spain, Thailand, Uganda and the West Indies. All the homes, everywhere, are practically autonomous and expected to be entirely self-supporting.

The whole organization developed and expanded not according to any pre-conceived plan, but as opportunity or need presented itself and normally in premises for which nobody else could find a use. The original basic aim was to care for the incurably disabled, those for whom hospitals could do nothing further and who had nowhere else suitable to go, but there are now also three homes for severely mentally retarded children and four hostels for adult, former mental hospital patients.

How this has all come about is typified in the story of Leslie Donovan. His wife developed multiple sclerosis and was taken into Le Court, where she stayed until her death. Leslie Donovan visited his wife constantly until the end. Some time later he married the then matron of Le Court. They lived in Hatfield, Hertfordshire, and spent the next four years raising no less than £85,000 to establish a specially built home at Hitchen. Not content with this, the Donovans went on to raise enough money to start another home at Parkstone, Poole, Dorset, to which Leslie's work had taken him. For two years Mr and Mrs Donovan ran the Parkstone home full-time.

Another example. A man was in a geriatric ward for more than ten years before a friend from the local Round Table organization decided to do something for him – and others. He assembled a small group of people who worked for five years, bought a house, repaired and decorated it, and housed ten disabled people. As a matter of policy, Cheshire Homes are kept to, at most, 35 residents, but about 20 is the preferred number since the great aim is to preserve a 'home' atmosphere, not an institutional one.

Each of the homes is managed by a committee drawn from the local community, all the members serving voluntarily. The central trust, the Cheshire Foundation Homes for the Sick, owns all the homes and assets and ensures the maintenance of standards, but otherwise there is a minimum of interference from headquarters. Each home receives grants from local authorities or regional hospital boards towards the care of individual residents but all capital costs have to be raised from charitable sources. The State pays, on average, about 70 per cent of the cost of keeping a resident and about 98 per cent of all residents are helped in this way.

In the homes there is generally a remarkable range of activities. The art is to give residents the greatest possible measure of freedom to help them live within the limits of their disabilities and up to the hilt of their capabilities. Cheshire Homes think first of the resident's residual powers – what capabilities they still retain – rather than what has been impaired or destroyed. Since the greatest wish of most disabled people is to be as independent as possible, to feel that they can still do something worthwhile, however small, are all encouraged to contribute something to the life and development of their new home. There is the usual occupational therapy craftwork; some people paint by using their feet or mouths; several have had books published; and others write television and radio plays. Residents at one home run a thriving duplicating service on commercial lines and quite a number of homes engage in different forms of factory out-work. Goods are produced for fêtes and sales of work and there is a shop, run by the residents, in almost every home. The residents themselves organize film shows and transport for outings. To sum up, the 21st anniversary international conference of Cheshire Foundations in July, 1969 approved this definition of a Cheshire Home wherever it might be: "A Cheshire Home should be a place of shelter physically, and of encouragement spiritually; a place in which the residents can acquire a sense of belonging and of ownership by contributing in any way within their capabilities to its functioning and development; a place to share with others, and from which to help others less fortunate; a place in which to gain confidence and develop independence and interests; a place of hopeful endeavour and not of passive disinterest."

In addition to raising money for their own local homes – or to start another one – the Support Groups, as they are called, help with the physical running of many homes: people go in to do the ironing and gardening, help with the cooking, serve meals, help paralysed or limbless residents, take people on outings, do the hair dressing and write letters for those who cannot do it for themselves.

Each home has a full-time staff in various categories but the needs are in many ways different from those of hospitals and nursing homes and to meet the special requirements of caring for the permanently disabled the Cheshire Foundation Service Corps was created; it provides an 18-months' course in residential care under a qualified tutorial staff.

In 1955 there were four homes in Britain and Cheshire certainly had no particular idea of starting more. But he was asked to go to India, where the need could be said to be greater than anything in Britain. So, at Christmas that year, he started a home in a tiny asbestos hut outside Bombay, without water or lighting. Today there are 17 homes in India alone. The overseas homes often concentrate on special categories of need, such as burnt-out leprosy cases, and destitute or handicapped children. Local communities start homes for whatever need is felt to be most urgent.

In countries without a national health service the Cheshire Homes face particular difficulties. Sometimes there is not even money for simple wheelchairs, and severely disabled people get around on their hands or in prams and pushchairs donated locally. Often the staff are unpaid. In 1959 Leonard Cheshire married Sue Ryder, who was herself celebrated for her work in bringing relief to survivors of Nazi persecution. Out of the combined work of the Sue Ryder Foundation and the Cheshire Foundation Homes there has evolved the Mission for the Relief of Suffering, of which the Missionaries of Charity – founded by Mother Teresa in Calcutta – is part. The mission is an association of separate and autonomous organizations, each devoted in its own way to the relief of suffering, but in some cases the organizations pool their resources and experience to meet specific and urgent needs that fall outside their own particular terms of reference.

The central organization of the Cheshire Foundation is, in some ways, as unusual as the whole concept. Presiding over everything is a central trust with a board of trustees, all of whom are professional men and women of high repute, each specially selected for some particular qualification and each already fully engaged in his or her own profession. The small headquarters office is served by a permanent staff of only seven, although half a dozen or so voluntary workers come in to help at various times each week. This headquarters is financed entirely by donations and legacies that come in centrally, not to any particular home. The donations have been declining somewhat of late – a sign of the times – but legacies, which range from £100 to £20,000, have shown a tendency to increase. It is the policy of the Foundation not to make national appeals. Each home is left to ask for funds in its own 'catchment area'. The task of raising money never ends . . . there are ten applications for every vacancy in a Cheshire home.

Broadly, money for the Cheshire Foundation seems to come in from the poor on the one hand and the wealthy on the other, but there is a certain amount of help from large companies, and other charities, notably the Spastics Society, help with money and specialized advice. Revenue has been rising steadily, but so have costs. The generally increased standards of living have called for ever-improved facilities in the homes and the Foundation says: "We encourage this because we think the disabled of the country have been third-class citizens long enough." The Foundation's central administrative costs are as low as two per cent, although, unlike other charities, the individual homes are not asked to contribute to headquarters' expenses. The administrative costs for the actual running of homes have been kept to an enviable 7.5 per cent, but this is only possible because of the tremendous amount of voluntary help. A lot of this help, both in time and money, comes from young people. For example, when the Foundation set out to establish a home for mentally retarded children of eleven upwards, much of the money came from a sponsored walk by pupils of Marlborough College.

Somewhat different from the usual Cheshire Home is the flats and bungalow centre at Tulse Hill in south London, built for families where someone is disabled. The idea is to provide the care and service that enables such families to stay together instead of the disabled member having to go into a residential home. The scheme is an outstanding example of a voluntary organization working with a local authority, in this case the Greater London Council, for the good of the community. The Greater London Council has built the housing and the Cheshire Foundation has provided about £45,000 for the construction of the nursing wing and a hall for work and recreation.

At 30 September 1971 the Foundation had total assets of £3,419,276, of which land, buildings and equipment represented just over £2m, and investments £392,399. Fees and grants from various authorities, from residents themselves and from other charities helping individual residents, totalled £1,172,933, but the cost of the homes for the year was £1,345,641. There was a deficit on maintenance of £351,877, all of which had to be raised from voluntary sources. The helpers covered the deficit more than twice over!

Subscriptions, donations and legacies to headquarters realized £603,337 and fêtes and other fund-raising efforts a further £152,765. At the end of the year the Foundation was able to transfer just over £400,000 to accumulated funds for expansion work. Investments and cash held by individual homes reached £780,000 compared with only £281,000 held by the central administration – of which £224,000 was committed to help individual homes, for extensions and improvements. This included £15,000 for overseas.

Finally in this story of charity work, a look at the grass roots, at a tiny local voluntary effort, small in comparison with the sums mentioned throughout this book, but an inspiring example of what goes on largely unseen, and how results can be achieved. It is also an example of caring until death.

The Southend & District Society for Mentally Handicapped Children began work in their Essex seaside town shortly after World War II as an informal group of parents who themselves had afflicted children. One of the original members described their aims thus: "I know for myself what a shattering experience it is to discover that your baby is mentally handicapped. We set out to show parents that they are not alone, that there are people at hand who have faced the same situation and are ready and willing to help, that friendship and the vital early assistance are available."

Today the society has some 300 members. In five years to early 1973 they raised about £15,000 for various projects and the society's general work, including £6,600 for an indoor swimming pool at a Southend school for mentally handicapped children from 2½ years upwards. It was one of the first societies in the country to provide a sheltered workshop to teach crafts and, in some cases sufficient skills to enable children to earn a living later in life.

But they did something else, perhaps far more important than just raising money. It is an example of co-operation between a local voluntary organization and the authorities that is rare, possibly unrivalled in the country. As soon as a new-born baby is found to be a mongol child – the largest single group of the mentally handicapped – a Southend Corporation medical officer visits the family with a member of the society who is herself the mother of a mongol boy or girl. The society points out that the birth of a mongol child is a time of terrible shock to the parents and no matter how kind and skilled are the doctors and the professional people around, 'something extra' is needed. That comes from the society members. The parents of the new, afflicted child can attend regular group meetings with other parents who have suffered like themselves; they can see that they are not alone; they can gain from the experience of the others.

This means that in the area, almost from birth and then as they grow up, the children are helped by devoted people, some as part of their job, others as a labour of love. The society supports a Southend school where the children can live in for occasional week-ends and for longer periods in the summer, which gives the parents a break from the continual, often almost unbearable strain imposed on family life by the constant attention such children require . . . and will need all their lives.

All their lives . . . yes, for the mind of a child born with a mental handicap will never develop, they never really grow up, they stay children till they die. That normally will be years after their parents have gone. The mother of one of Southend's mongol girls, a member of the society, put the great problem this way:

> My husband and I joined the local society and the help this brought was immeasurable. One of the most heartening experiences was finding there were so many other parents like ourselves. It removed the sense of isolation, the burden of being 'different'. Now that our daughter is growing up we can look back almost with surprise at our earlier fears. She is learning to take her place in the community, accepted by our friends and developing a charming and endearing personality of her own. Over the years we have learned many lessons. She has taught us patience, tolerance and a new set of values. Because of her steady progress, the help

of the local society and the companionship of other parents like ourselves, we should look to the future with hope.

But one dark shadow looms. It is the thought that constantly haunts every parent of a mentally handicapped child – and a day never passes when I do not ask myself the chilling question: 'What is to be become of my daughter when we are no longer here? Who will house her, protect her and care for her needs? Where will she go? . . . Who will want her?

The Southend & District Society for Mentally Handicapped Children set out to do something about that dark shadow. They launched a drive to collect money for a residential home where mentally handicapped children who have lost their parents or can no longer stay with them may live. The society had something over £7,000 in hand, raised over two and a half years, and now set out to bring that to £35,000 to build a home with eight single bedrooms, special bathrooms, and a flat for the house parents. They produced about 250 copies of a four-page leaflet, eloquently explaining what they wanted to do. They showed clearly what everything was going to cost: a bedroom £850, a recreation room £3,000, a washing machine £100, a radiator £40, and so on. Southend Corporation, which will eventually run the home, gave the land, the site of an ancient Saxon settlement at Shoeburyness on the Thames estuary.

In a year £8,000 was raised in cash and various people and organizations are pledged to pay for individual things or sections of the building. Typical is the response from the Southend branch of the Customs and Excise, who have promised £900 towards the cost of central heating, and are sending it in to the society at the rate of £100 a month.

The whole operation is a perfect example of helping to fill one of the gaps in the Welfare State, of doing what Governments do not, and of approaching it the right way – by telling people exactly what is needed and why, and precisely where the money will be spent. Nor are there any heavy administration costs: nobody connected with the society in any way is paid a penny. A home for just eight children is in truth small but it is not insignificant. It is a beginning, an attack on that dark shadow that hovers over about one in a hundred of all babies born in the United Kingdom each year, and their parents.

Once again, love shows the way.

INDEX